HEALTH COACHING BUSINESS

how to built a passion in a profitable business

WARREN DYLOG

© Copyright 2019
By WARREN DYLOG

All rights reserved.

This document is geared towards providing exact and reliable information with regards to the topic and issue covered. The publication is sold with the idea that the publisher is not required to render accounting, officially permitted, or otherwise, qualified services. If advice is necessary, legal or professional, a practiced individual in the profession should be ordered.

-From a Declaration of Principles which was accepted and approved equally by a Committee of the American Bar Association and a Commit
tee of Publishers and Associations.

In no way is it legal to reproduce, duplicate, or transmit any part of this document in either electronic means or in printed format. Recording of this publication is strictly prohibited and any storage of this document is not allowed unless with written permission from the publisher. All rights reserved.

The information provided herein is stated to be truthful and consistent, in that any liability, in terms of inattention or otherwise, by any usage or abuse of any policies, processes, or directions contained within is the solitary and utter responsibility of the recipient reader. Under no circumstances will any legal responsibility or blame be held against the publisher for any reparation, damages, or monetary loss due to the information herein, either directly or indirectly.

Respective authors own all copyrights not held by the publisher.

The information herein is offered for informational purposes solely, and is universal as so. The presentation of the information is without contract or any type of guarantee assurance.

The trademarks that are used are without any consent, and the publication of the trademark is without permission or backing by the trademark owner.

All trademarks and brands within this book are for clarifying purposes only and are the owned by the owners themselves, not affiliated with this document.

Table of Contents

What Is Health Coaching?........................1

   Health And Wellness Coaching 3

   Health Coaching: Changing The Way We Get Healthy 6

   Musings From a Health Coach.............9

   How to Become a Health Coach........14

   Tips in Health Coach Training 16

   Health Coaching - Top 10 Reasons to Hire Or Be One 19

   Health Coach Training For a Healthier Life...27

   Health Coaches: What a Coconut Can Teach You About Charging and Amp - Getting Paid What You're Worth 31

   Use Content To Grow Your Health Coaching Practice - Enhance Your Expert Status...35

   What Makes a Good Health Coach? .40

   The Basics Behind Health Coaching Certification Programs 43

Is Certified Health Coach Training in Your Future?..46

Coaching Business - A Way to a Healthy Body and Successful Life 49

Health Coaching - The Key to Replacing Bad Habits With Good 51

Healthy Living & Lifestyle: Health Coaching: Invest in Your Future - Stop Sabotaging Your Life.............................55

Are You Ready to Start Your Coaching Business? 58

Things to Do Before Building Your Coaching Business 61

Coach - Are You Interested in Growing Your Coaching Business - Or Are You Stopping New Clients 67

Starting a Coaching Business - FAQ's Answered 74

5 Things You Can Do Right Now to Jump-Start Your Coaching Business....77

How to Grow Your Coaching Business Using VIP Packages 80

Marketing Your Coaching Business Successfully 86

How Can You Run a Successful Coaching Business? 90

How To Build Your Coaching Business With Testimonials 94

The Ten Keys to Building Your Coaching Business Beyond the Next Level 100

How Can A Health Coach Help Me? 120

Health and Wellness Coaching - What's All This Stuff About? 122

Health and Wellness Coach Training 125

What Can Health and Wellness Coaching Do For You? 128

Finding Out What's Right for YOU - Health Coaching 131

Health Coaching: Internet-Based Marketing Strategy for Modern Dinosaurs 134

Realizing Health-Oriented Goals Through Health Coaching 137

Health Coaching - The Real Deal 140

Build Your Health Coaching Business Like You Would Your Home 143

Build Your Coaching Business - You Are Uniquely Qualified For This - Discovery of the Unique You 146

Building Your Coaching Business on What Works - Not What Doesn't 149

Inspiration Vs Motivation Applied To Building Your Health Coaching Business .. 156

Can You Benefit From Health Coaching? 158

The Benefits of a Health Coach 163

Health Coach Salary: How Much Does a Health and Wellness Coach Make a Year? 167

Conclusion 171

What Is Health Coaching?

We all know how important our health is. We are what we eat, and as we grow older, the condition of our body deteriorates and we must take good care of our body. Many health experts have advised people that they should not smoke, eat more greens and vegetables and also to exercise regularly. However, even though many people are told to do such things over and over again, they fail to listen to these good instructions and only regret in the latter part of their lives. Well, perhaps one of the ways out of this is to engage a health coach.

Let me first define what health coaching is. Health coaching is employing a health coach, or if possible coaching yourself through some personal coaching, such that you obtain some guidance on how to improve your health. This also includes addressing your own health needs and making changes to your behaviors to improve your health. Like traditional forms of coaching such as life coaching, health coaches would formulate goals to reach certain health targets with their clients. This also includes the identification of obstacles and the use of personal support systems. The relationship between the coach and client hinges on accountability. The coach would also focus the client and lead him to achieve what was set by his healthcare practitioners as the overall health outcome goals.

There is also some history of health coaching. Health coaching began with psychologists treating persons addicted to alcohol in the early 1990s. Then, the National Institute on Alcohol Abuse and Alcoholism conducted a study that compared several methods of treatment for alcohol addiction. The findings revealed that while many of the methods used to treat alcohol abuse were equally effective, motivational interviewing was more cost-effective and timelier in reaching the desired results. This has led researchers to be more interested to use this approach. They now study how such motivational interviewing can be used to affect health behavior changes in persons with chronic conditions.

While the traditional approach to patient teaching and education is to give information to the patient, health coaching or motivational interviewing, on the other hand, involves engaging a health coach to guide the patient to talk about what is most troubling to them about their conditions, what they most want to change, what support they have to foster change, and what obstacles or difficulties must be removed or minimized to advance healthy behaviors.

Health And Wellness Coaching

"Health is a state of complete physical, mental and social well-being, and not merely the absence of disease or infirmity." (World Health Org., 1948). Health and wellness coaching is a result-oriented process designed to help individuals meet the challenges and demands of 21st-century living. Coaching helps you jump the hurdles and obstacles in your life, stay focused, develop positive mental skills for creating change, and move forward with energy and hopefulness.

Coaching is not psychotherapy. As Judy Rosemarin, a coaching teacher at New York University's Center for Career Education, says, "Psychotherapy is looking through the rear-view mirror at life, and coaching is looking through the front windshield." A coach is someone who motivates you, provides support, identifies strengths and obstacles, and partners with you to plan creative solutions you need to reach your goals.

A coach works with you through skillfully conducted "coaching sessions," using any combination of planned activities, hand-selected educational resources, and methods such as active imagery, restructuring negative beliefs, encouragement, personal development, and venting.

You can talk with your coach about whatever is needed to help you take action and produce results. You might focus on goals, strategies, and establishing boundaries; set up systems to assure that you stay motivated; strengthen other areas of your life that serve as the basis for change; develop a plan to establish the necessary support network and environment to assure your success; implement methods to avoid relapse; identify stale habits and mindsets that you must let go of so that you can excel; find new ways to create the time and energy you require; celebrate your accomplishments; and reverse your setbacks. However, keep in mind that much of your progress is measured between sessions when you implement the actions that will most likely lead to the positive results you want.

True health--or what we commonly call "wellness"--is a dynamic state of vitality and physical, mental, emotional, and spiritual well-being. It does not occur through a focus on alleviating disease, but rather occurs when you commit proactively to a focus on health and wellness. In wellness, the focus is on supporting your core being and vitality. As you optimize your health and wellness, you will be better able to handle the stress of day to day living, leading to a reduction in stress-related illnesses and setting the stage for healing to occur. Health and wellness coaching topics include identifying stressors, creating a complete health/wellness vision, identifying key motivators to change, identifying roadblocks to change, identifying successes, creating pathways around barriers, stress management, using adversity as an advantage, and building upon natural strengths, skills, and abilities.

Coaching is effective in this process due to its focus on both short- and long-term goals, the use of written commitments to fulfill the action plan, tracking progress and holding the client accountable to those commitments, and providing a structured and supportive environment. Individuals who benefit include those who need motivation, discipline, or accountability to meet their goals; those who need a personalized plan that meets and evolves with their unique needs; and those who want the privacy and confidentiality provided by their coach.

Your coach will form a powerful alliance with you to both guide and facilitate you in a dynamic process of positive change, assisting you, for example, in your efforts to lose weight, control pain, manage blood sugars, control blood pressure, and reduce stress. The ultimate result of this partnership is improved health, a boost in energy and positive outlook, and a more balanced approach to life. The main goal is typically to empower clients to facilitate their healthy lifestyle changes through a directive, individualized, structured program that includes ongoing assessment of quantifiable goals and necessary corrective modifications to treatment.

Health Coaching: Changing The Way We Get Healthy

It seems that given enough time almost all things in life will change. Whether it be the change in appearance, change in value, or simply change in definition. And if you've surpassed your teenage years you know this all too well. Which depending upon how far past your teenage years you are, your level of the first-hand experience will vary. But most people that have made it through their teenage years though, have lived long enough to see a pretty substantial amount of change in the world. Whether it be in fashion, music, or entertainment. You've probably also seen a lot of change in the health industry as well when it comes to how we get healthy. From Richard Simmons to Jenny Craig. In more recent years there has been yet another shift in the health industry. Specifically in the area of how people are pursuing getting healthy.

This shift is being spurred on by a variety of factors. Not limited to but including a growing field of coaches. And we're not talking about the coaches that are teaching your kid's soccer and football teams on the weekends but rather a different type of coach called a Health Coach. A coach that does so much more than teach you the proper technique for bench press or the appropriate foods to consume throughout your day. These Health Coaches are teaching their clients how to set goals, identify their values, and most importantly all change their behaviors. After all, the reality is that our behaviors (choices) are directly tied to our overall health. If our behaviors aren't conducive for a healthy living then we will reap the consequences of them. And vice versa, if our behaviors are wise and smart when it comes to things affecting our health then we will reap the rewards of those positive behaviors.

The problem is that many people don't know how to go about changing their behaviors. They may succeed for some time but inevitably fall back in the same rut that they were in before. Or they just simply don't know how to keep themselves motivated and therefore after a few weeks or months, find themselves back in square one. Gym clubs see this occur every single year in January. People make new year's resolutions to get healthy and start extremely motivated. Which is why gyms are always extremely crowded in January. But within a short period that initial momentum fizzles out and they stop going to the Gym. And many times it's not due to lack of desire to become healthier but rather could probably be better attributed to the lack of knowledge they have in knowing how to change the behaviors that are prohibiting them from becoming healthier. That's where the Health Coach comes in.

Health Coaches are changing the way people get healthy by providing them that knowledge and ability to change their behaviors. And it isn't coming in the form of textbook knowledge as you would think but rather it's coming in the form of helping the person to better understand their internal thought process and promoting positive thinking which in turn spawns motivation. That motivation then helps the behavior changes persist not just for a short period but permanently. With the result being a person that is equipped with the necessary knowledge and motivation to maintain healthy behaviors and not just be another new year's resolution gym member that fizzles out in a few weeks.

Musings From a Health Coach

I'll begin with a conversation I had with a student just this past week. A female in her early 30s, let's call her Joe, signed up for the health coach training program, not to become a health coach, but simply to learn how to live a healthier life. However, as she moved through the program Joe became a little more open to the idea of health coaching and has just recently signed on a client. Unfortunately, just a few days after signing the client, the client called Joe to say that she was reconsidering the health coaching program for financial reasons. So Joe began to doubt the worth of she is offering as a health coach, just as any new health coach would after having a client cancel their program. During our call last week, Joe started asking me questions like, "What am I providing for the client? Why is it valuable? Do I have something of worth to offer them if it's nothing physical that they are getting from me?"

Of course, there may be many reasons that someone would back out of working with a health coach before their program has begun. If a client backs out because of finances after already committing to the program, one reason could be that they don't know or understand everything that a health coach can provide for them. They understand it in theory, but they don't feel it and they can't imagine how great it could be. I want to focus on this potential situation in particular because it is easy to avoid with a little practice.

The average person has forgotten what it feels like to have a health professional fully committed to spending a significant amount of time on them. They have forgotten that someone could be physically, mentally and emotionally focused on them for longer than 5 minutes! When a health coach sits down with a client, the cell phone goes off, there are no televisions in sight and the door is closed. No one is leaving or coming. Health coach and client face each other seated, in comfortable chairs with a notepad and glass of water, and they talk. They work through the challenges that interrupt a healthy, balanced lifestyle and they create solutions so that the client may move forward with his or her goals and dreams. Even if the potential client does understand this, sometimes they still can't see the benefit because they have never had someone do this for them.

All that being said, there is a solution!

It simply takes more of an effort to help your prospective client see what you can do for them.

I know two specific "tricks" that you can use to overcome this health coaching challenge and I think that as you read them, your faith in the value of your service will be reaffirmed.

First of all, you need to tweak your initial conversation with the potential client. There are two steps to take during an initial consultation that I believe are essential. The first step is to summarize their health challenges and/or goals after taking their health history.

This step helps to establish trust between client and coach and to remind them of what it feels like to have someone listen and hear them.

Then right after you summarize their specific health challenges and/or goals, you ask the magic question. That question is, "How do you want my support with reaching these health goals (or, with overcoming these health challenges)?"

Sometimes they will have no idea how to answer this question. You can clarify by giving them examples of how you could support them, like by talking through the problem with them, taking them grocery shopping, giving them private cooking lessons, trouble-shooting when they can't figure out how to fit more greens in their diet, organizing their pantry, teaching them about nutrition, etc.

The point is that they need to verbalize how they want you to support them with reaching their health goals and you need to confirm that that is what you can and want to do for them.

Don't forget to give them some examples of what you will do together, ask them if they have any specific requests, and take notes!

My second thought on how to help a potential client

see the worth of your service is less specific but even more important. It has to do with your confidence level.

For a person to want to trust you with their future, they have to respect you. It almost verges on the point of them needing to idolize you. They need to want what you have. This is a very subtle, instinctual and possibly unconscious feeling that they get about you based on your feelings about yourself. Some of the time you cannot control this, but most of the time you can.

One way you can improve your confidence in yourself and your service is to practice talking to people. Practice asking them questions and try to get them to talk about their personal life. They won't know what you're doing and you will become very skilled at making someone comfortable with opening up to you and getting them into the right mindset to say "yes!" to working with you. I believe that once you start putting those suggestions into practice, you will begin to believe that the work you do is invaluable, as will your potential clients.

How to Become a Health Coach

Preventative health is a much smarter approach to being healthy as opposed to having a curative approach. It's much more difficult and expensive to restore health than it is to maintain. Health coaching is becoming a growing career field that has been enjoying a lot of acclaim in recent media stories. Paul Zane Pilzer is a New York Times selling author who once predicted that health and wellness would soon be a trillion-dollar industry. His prediction seems to be accurate.

Successful health and wellness coaches should be naturally health conscious. Committing to eating healthy, living a healthy lifestyle and maintaining a degree of fitness should be a priority. Clients naturally want to hire health and wellness coaches who walk their walk and talk their talk.

To evaluate whether becoming a health coach would be a good career, do some research in regards to salary, hours, and opportunities which are currently offered to health coaches. Interview local health and wellness coaches to determine the climate in your area for that field. Evaluate the demographics and economy of the area to determine if a health and wellness related business might have a good chance of being successful. Consider whether residents of your area are health conscious and have disposable income.

Most health and wellness coaches work for themselves in the form of private practice. This requires having solid business skills and experience. Organizational habits, marketing strategies, and determination would also be helpful.

Many schools offer certification for health and wellness coaches. Some schools offer distance learning, while others offer online classes or weekend attendance. Look closely at several schools and compare their qualifications, tuition, and the success of their graduates.

Contact local colleges to evaluate their programs as well. Options would include getting a degree in dietetics, public health, and other fields such as counseling, psychology or sociology.

The most important strategy when evaluating a school is to search for graduates from the health coach school you are considering to get opinions on current student's and graduates' experience and get recommendations they might have.

Ask about the experience they may have already had with their health coaching career and find out what type of career options they have discovered. You can also inquire politely about the income they've received as a health coach. Some health and wellness coaching schools offer discounts to friends and family of alumni, which could be an added benefit to contacting a recent grad of a nutrition school you are considering.

Tips in Health Coach Training

Health coach training is a good investment if you want a long career in the health and wellness industry. This industry is slowly growing as one of the most fulfilling and profitable industries today. More and more people are becoming aware of the importance of preventative health and are engaging in health and wellness and may need health coaches along the way.

Health coach training prepares you to become a person of authority when it comes to good health. It is a rapidly growing career and is predicted to become a trillion-dollar industry over the next few years. If you are interested in keeping yourself healthy and fit, it would be wise to train to be a health coach to learn more about the natural strategies of living a healthy and long life.

- The first step in becoming an effective and successful health coach is to live a healthy life. If you are healthy and fit, you become more credible and efficient in teaching others to follow the healthy lifestyle that you live yourself. Walk the walk and talk the talk and you will soon learn ways of not just keeping yourself healthy but also other people that you deal with as a health coach.

- When you decide to become a health coach, make sure that you have the qualities that it takes to become one. Being a wellness coach requires you to have compassion, patience and a sincere desire to help other people achieve good health and the happiness that comes with it. If you are caring by nature, then you might have a shot at being a good wellness coach.

- Being a wellness coach is also not just all about philanthropy, it is also a business and a source of income. Before engaging in the field of health counseling, determine the salary range that you could expect to make in a month. You can't just offer your services for free and it takes a lot of hard work too so make sure that you are paid for what you and your services are worth.

- Do some research with health coaches in your area and ask the amount of salary that you could expect when you enter this business. Consider the demographics of your area, the economy, the population and other factors that may affect your health counseling venture. Being a wellness coach also re*q*uires financial investment so make sure that you can expect a return or revenue in your area.

- If you think that being a wellness coach is lucrative and fulfilling, you can jumpstart your career in many ways. A lot of coaches work in private practice and only for themselves. If you feel that you are *q*ualified and you have a good business background, you can use your marketing knowledge to build a name for yourself as a wellness coach.

To build credibility, you should engage in considerable training and attend schools that will give you a certification. Certifications will not only train you on how to become a good wellness coach, but it is also a good addition to your resume.

Health Coaching - Top 10 Reasons to Hire Or Be One

Health Coaching is a relatively new profession that focuses on helping people make positive changes in their health, physical, mental and emotional lives, that they have not been able to do for themselves. It's about people deciding that the personal cost for not making some changes has become too high. They are willing to trade pain for gain -- so to speak. Here are ten "pain for gain" reasons to hire (or become) a health coach.

- **Health Coaching and Weight Loss**

  One of the most challenging (and discouraging) behavioral changes that people try to make is losing weight and keeping it off. We are all aware of the health risks associated with being overweight. Many people have been on the weight loss and gain it back yo-yo ride for years. What can make the difference and break this vicious cycle is a trained professional to guide you on how to take it off and keep it off. This can be done with a few key lifestyle changes which are easier than you might think especially with the support of a health coach. What would it mean to you to lose 20-40 pounds and never gain it back? Visualize yourself at your ideal weight. What does that feel like? What does it look like? See yourself there now. Feels great, doesn't it?

- **Health Coaching and Eating Habits**

A second behavior change that is tied to and often more challenging than weight loss is our eating habits. We love to eat (and eat and eat and eat) And most of us are addicted to some form of junk food. Mine is chocolate. How our lives could change if we could make a few basic improvements in our daily diet. More energy, better sleep, less illness because of a boosted immune system, healthier skin, look better, feel better. So how do we do it? A health coach can introduce and effective program that makes sense and is easy to do if you are motivated to make a few changes and reap the rewards.

- **Health Coaching and Stress**

Stress can destroy people's lives. The pace today is hectic and people are paying the price. Marital breakups, illness, child abuse, addictions, mental ill-health, low self-esteem, the list is endless. The price is high and robs us of *q*uality of life... We live a fast-paced life with multiple responsibilities. Learning to manage stress can save your life. What a different life you could lead if you could tame the tiger and learn to channel stressful events so they worked for you rather than against you. A health coach can show you how to do that.

- **Health Coaching and Positive Relationships**

Positive nurturing relationships are vital to a healthy life. How well we get along with others including our own family often will determine our level of emotional and mental health. Lots of people are challenged in this area because they have not learned the social skills it takes. Ongoing conflict with people at work or home can and not knowing "how to fix it" can compromise your quality of life. The solutions to this kind of difficulties are easier than you might think. There a few "learnable" skills that can make a huge difference in your relationships. Ask yourself what it would mean to you to have much more positive and enjoyable communication and relationships with someone at work, your family, your spouse or your kids. Health coaching can make a difference.

- **Health Coaching and Communication Skills**

I hear this all the time. 'We can't communicate, we argue all the time, he/she doesn't listen to me, we're not on the same page, I wish I could tell him what I think, I just don't know what to say. Perhaps one of the greatest failures of our educational system is not teaching basic communication skills, how to connect with people, how to listen, how to say what you think or feel so people will listen. Probably the #1 reason for failed relationships is people not knowing how to communicate effectively with each other. There are basic effective easy to learn talking and listening skills that would resolve most misunderstandings and health coaching can teach you them easily and *q*uickly.

- **Health Coaching and Exercise**

Exercise. A four-letter word for some. The fact is just a little more routine exercise in our daily lives could have a significant impact on our health. I like to walk and jog and lift light weights. It could be bike riding, swimming or flopping on the floor during commercials and doing some light stretching. A lack of exercise can ruin your health. A health coach can get you started towards a more active existence and help you stick with it long enough for it to make a significant difference. Go for it.

- **Health Coaching - Preventative vs. Curative**

A distinct advantage of health coaching is that it is preventative as opposed to curative. Would you rather have someone help you prevent diabetes or some other debilitating disease or visit a doctor to get treated after the fact? That is the choice a lot of people are facing but the point is you have a choice and if you don't choose for yourself, life will choose for you. Make a wise choice and choose the path of prevention. You will reap the rewards of better health and health coaching can get you there.

- **Health Coach - Being a Role Model**

Be a trendsetter, be a role model for others. Just think of the impact you could have on other people's lives especially those you care about most. What if because of changes YOU made your mother, father, sister, brother, child or friend made a significant change in their health. What would that feel like? You often see people make dramatic changes after the heart attack. Well, those same changes can be made right now and have the effect of preventing a disastrous heart attack or stroke. What if because of the changes you made it prevented a family member or friend from having a serious illness. This scenario is *q*uite possible. Because I have started to run regularly both my kids and my wife have started walk/jogging. What a thrill for me. Who knows how that will benefit them in the years to come. So be a trendsetter in your family. Your family will love you for it and you will feel great about yourself for doing it.

- **Health Coaching and Self Esteem**

A lasting benefit of health coaching is how you feel about yourself when you succeed at making important changes in your health. This is because of the positive feelings and feedback you get from family and friends (and when you look in the mirror). You've lost weight and people notice and comment. You're not as stressed out and it feels good. You have more energy and you are more active. You're sleeping better and you look more rested. Your relationship with your spouse and kids has improved. People around you will often mirror your mood and energy. You're more fun to be around, not as irritable, short-tempered or demanding. Your doctor notices and commends you for your efforts. You just feel good about yourself and you're not going back to the way it was. Never!!

- **Health Coaching - It Could Be For You**

One of the things that happen for some who go through health coaching and derive significant benefits from it, is they get exposed to the process and see how much it benefits others and how it could be a powerful change agent for people 'stuck in the muck' and suffering the consequences. It can often influence them enough to consider being a health coach themselves. Health coaching is a rapidly growing profession and is open to most people as an income choice, part time or full time, who have a genuine interest and desire to help others. Not to mention that the average hourly for a session ranges from 100 to 200 dollars for a session. A rather 'healthy' income.

So in summary, these are just a few of the benefits for hiring (or becoming) a health coach. Decide that you deserve excellent vibrant health and if you can't achieve it on your own or would like to speed up the process consider hiring a health coach. A healthier, happier life awaits you.

Health Coach Training For a Healthier Life

Health Coaching... getting your wellness coach certification... is one of the fastest-growing income opportunities both online and offline today. And here's why:

When you look around, what do you see? The majority of us are addicted to fast foods. On a recent trip to my sister's place, a 7-hour journey, we counted 178 Fast Food outlets along the highway.

I heard a statistic recently that claimed that 3 out of 4 people in the USA are either pre-diabetic or close to it. Obesity is rampant. Even childhood obesity is rampant. Our food choices are often high fat and highly unhealthy. We are digging our graves with our teeth. Health care costs are skyrocketing. People NEED good information about their health, and with a certification in health coaching, you can provide that to them!

Look around at your own family, friends or people you work with. People in their 40's, 50's, and 60's are beginning to pay a serious price with illness and a compromised lifestyle. And these are people you know and care about. Have you ever thought that YOU can help these folks?

Well, by becoming a certified health coach... you can!

Health Coaching is one way we can reverse this trend. People helping people at the grassroots level, one bad habit, one step at a time. People can be empowered to make better choices and have better health without having to get sick first. That is exactly what health coach training enables people to do for others.

Health Coach Training--The Difference Maker

Here are 5 key reasons why people choose health coaching as an income generator for themselves.

- **Health Coaching makes a difference in people's lives.**

Can you imagine what it would feel like to help someone you know or care about, make a significant permanent change in their life? How gratifying would that be? You now have a job that changes people's lives and you get to do that on a day to day basis.

- **Health Coaching -- Change Your Financial Picture**

People choose health coaching as a way to significantly improve their financial situation. The average rate for a session ranges from $120/hr to $190/hr. A 10 hr week would generate an extra 5 to $6,000 a month income, an amount that would make a huge difference in most people's lives. You can see how you could easily build this into a six-figure income for yourself.

- **Health Coaching -- A Transitional Career Choice**

Many people will fit those 10 hours into their existing careers or jobs. People already in the health profession often see health coaching as an easy fit with their current training and job. They can offer it as additional service to their existing clientele or build a part-time caseload and earn extra income. Some use it as a transition from what they are doing now to a full-time career that is more lucrative and rewarding. Many health care jobs are high stress, routine with mediocre pay and no job security.

- **Health Coaching-- The Road to Security and Freedom**

Perhaps just as exciting for people than the potential six-figure income is to be able to have control over their own lives. One of the things that cause people great stress and unhappiness is having to go to work even if you or your children are not well to a job that brings you very little self-satisfaction and a pay level which dictates their lifestyle, week after week, month after month, year after year. Health coaching can change that for you. You get to choose. You can have control over how many hours you work, who you work with, when you go on vacation, for how long. You can schedule your appointments around important family events. You can put your health and the health of your family first. You get your life back.

- **Get Started and Get Going - Get Your Wellness Coach Certification**

A major reason people choose health coaching is that it is easy to learn to do. Attend classes online, on your computer and every facet of starting a business will be taught to you. This is something most people can do if they have the interest and are motivated to take control of their own lives. If you enjoy working with people and have at least average communication skills, the rest you will learn over several months. And you can earn as you learn. You will be supervised every step of the way as you begin your health coaching business.

So check this out for yourself. It could be exactly what you've been looking for.

Health Coaches: What a Coconut Can

Teach You About Charging and Amp - Getting Paid What You're Worth

I was just opening a young coconut with a corkscrew, and boy is my wrist sore! Most coconuts open up immediately when I use a corkscrew to dig a hole so I can stick my straw in it. This one was taking so long and required digging in 4 different areas! It was a huge ordeal- I had to put my whole weight on the area where I was corkscrewing it open. I started to get hot and felt like I was working out.

At that moment, I was thinking to myself that I wished I got the coconut from Whole Foods instead. You see, Whole Foods sells fresh young coconuts for $2.99 and has a hole already dug in it, plus they provide you with a straw you can pull out of a container when you decide to buy the coconut. I buy my young coconuts from an Asian grocery store that sells them for $1.85 without the straw. Whole Foods' young coconuts (the same brand) are a 60% markup from the Asian grocery store! Sixty percent. And I see people buy it day in and day out.

As a holistic health practitioner, this is what you can

learn from Whole Foods: take something that is the same thing other places sell, add value to it, and charge more for it. People buy the coconut with a hole in it for a % markup and they gladly pay it, so they don't need to have sore wrists like me. One fear holistic health practitioners share with me about charging more is that they are afraid people will stop using their services. An acupuncturist I was talking to last week said he lowered his fees because people said they were too much. He's afraid of increasing them now because he's worried his patients will leave.

The problem is when you raise your prices, do you also add more value (or perceived value)? Yes, prices may be adjusted for inflation with reason. But if you offer the same thing at a significantly higher price, inevitably, some people will not come back. The *q*uestion is… what can you do to offer a higher perceived value?

One way is to explain what you do to potential clients in a way that highlights more value. This can be done by focusing on sharing the benefits of what a potential client would experience by working with you, rather than focusing on the process they would experience. For example, instead of just telling a potential client that during a reflexology session they would experience a foot massage, say something like "you'll feel more relaxed from the stress you've been feeling all week, toxins will be eliminated, you may experience better sleep and balance of your digestives [or whatever other problem your client may be experiencing]. Another way to charge more is to add more value. What can you do to add more value without it taking much more of your time?

This is something I work on with my private clients and which makes a huge difference in making more income in their practice. We work on re-designing the way they offer their current services. Then we package it and market the services more attractively, justifies a higher value, and charge more for it. It allows them to charge a lot more without having to work harder. And their patients/clients don't mind it, because they appreciate more value (perceived and/or actual). Now, during the in-between period, you may lose some of your current patients/clients. At the same time, you may start attracting patients/clients you want to work with and who can afford your services.

What would it be like for you if you could start charging more and only work with the patients/clients you most enjoy working with? Would you make a more consistent income? Do you think you'll enjoy your practice more, and your clients would appreciate you more because you're not so burned out? Reflect on what you can do to start charging more for your naturopathic, chiropractic, acupuncturist, health/ spiritual coach, or massage therapy practice. And if you have any tips on how to open up a young coconut without breaking your wrist or exerting all your energy, do share by contacting me! I'm addicted to them and drink them every day…

Use Content To Grow Your Health Coaching Practice - Enhance Your Expert Status

Why do you want to position yourself as an expert? Because people look for experts to solve a particular problem, people have more trust in experts, and people are willing to pay more for experts.

Luckily, you don't have to spend more time and money to get more letters behind your name before others consider you as an expert. Whether you are perceived as an expert depends on a large part of how you position yourself - and creating content in your area of specialty is an excellent way of putting yourself in front of your target market as an expert.

Here Are A Few Ways That You Can Leverage Content To Build Your Expert Status:

- **Blog**

Posting on your blog regularly is, in my opinion, the easiest and fastest way to accumulate a body of content that will help position you as an expert. The key is to focus on the area of your specialty, go deep and provide relevant and valuable information. Do not write about everything and anything - you may have more people reading your posts at the beginning, but it will do nothing to help you reach your target market - it's like throwing spaghetti on the wall and hoping something will stick - not effective.

Guest blogging is another great way to expend your reach and put your expertise in front of more people. Select websites that share your target audience to contribute to. Make sure you include in your submission a bio - a brief description of your services and your expertise and let people know how to find you by including your website URL. You can also use this an opportunity to grow your list by directing people to sign up for your gift - which is another way to grow your business with content.

- **eBook**

Having a "book" is a great way to boost your expert status. The good news is, you don't have to start from scratch. Pick a topic that resonates with your target audience, create an outline, and then look through your blog posts, articles, and anything else you have written. You should be able to compile this content together to form a good part of the book. Now you can see what you are missing and create content to fill in the blanks.

- **Video**

Video with content covering your area of specialty not only positions you as an expert but also increases the "like, know and trust" factor by giving your audience a face and a voice to relate to. You can create video from your blog post content, or you can do "video blog". Don't worry about having a lot to say - in fact, you want to keep it short and sweet so that your audience will actually watch your video (for me, I usually just file the item under "to catch up later" if the video is too long - which of course, rarely gets watched). When you post your video on YouTube (you should, it's the second most searched site on the interwebs), make sure you include relevant keywords indicating your area of expertise so that people can find you.

- **Information Products**

When you share your knowledge using an information product, people would see you as an expert because you are teaching something. If you have been writing and talking about your topic of expertise for a while, you probably don't have to start from scratch. Pick a hot topic, create an outline, and then look through the content that you have already created. Compile your existing content and then you will be able to see what materials you need to generate to fill the gap.

- **Info Flyer for Referral Partners**

Your referral partners are probably regarded as an expert by their clients or patients. If they share the information written by you with their clients, you will very likely be considered as an authority. You can appropriate your existing content, such as blog post, into a flyer format, which you can distribute to your partners to share with their clients. You are helping them add value to what they are giving their clients while positioning yourself as a resource for their clients (your potential clients). Don't forget to add some information about your services on these flyers - your area of expertise, information about your services, how to learn more and how to contact you.

You don't have to create fresh content for each of these media - people who see your videos may not come across your blog posts. Your eBooks and your information products can be a compilation of your best blog posts on a specific topic - most people would not have read all your blog posts, and even if they do, they would appreciate having all the relevant information in one place in the case of an ebook, or paired with additional information and resources in the case of an information product.

Don't be shy - look through what you have and you will be surprised how much you have to share!

What Makes a Good Health Coach?

There are of course many qualities that make a person a good health coach. While it certainly makes sense for someone already in the health and wellness industry, it is not necessarily a requirement to become a health coach.

This article discusses some of the basic qualities of what makes a person a good health or wellness coach, regardless of his/her background.

One such quality is the ability to empathetically communicate with people. Empathetic communication will encourage the client to accept you as a trusted health coach. What this means is that the health coach can identify with the feelings, thoughts, or attitudes of his client. Using empathy may lead to an improved relationship between the health coach and client.

Another quality that is related to empathetic communication is to listen, actually to listen effectively. A coach needs to be trained to listen effectively since people vary in their communication skills. Some clients may express themselves clearly while others may not. A coach needs to be aware of the different needs of his/her client base and how the coach/client communication and listening skills affect the interaction.

The wellness coach has to leave his personal opinions out of the coaching session. The coach needs to be completely non-judgmental. The wellness coach absolutely should not judge his/her client based on his standards or opinions. Much of a coach's training will be on how to be aware of this and to have the self-control to NOT allow his personal opinions to be communicated.

Another fundamental quality of a health coach is the integrity to keep all information about the client confidential. The coach/client relationship is based on trust and the client must be sure that the coach can be trusted with private matters.

Also, the coach still must be somewhat of a mentor,

guidance counselor, and cheerleader all wrapped up in one! The health coach should allow the client some flexibility in the agenda of each session, but the coach should also guide the session conversation so that it is an effective one. The client sets his/her own goals, again with the guidance from the coach. The coach may challenge the client a bit if the goals are too vague or too big. In the latter case, the coach may suggest smaller "bite-size" goals so that the client has a better chance of reaching those goals. Of course, all successes are celebrated.

In summary, there are many qualities that a health coach should have and there are also many roles that he/she has. Each coaching relationship will be different and the wellness coach will need to be a bit flexible. A coaching relationship can in some cases grow into a life-long friendship as well.

The Basics Behind Health Coaching Certification Programs

A health coach is often employed by a person who has some type of chronic illness. This isn't always the case though, sometimes people need a coach to guide them through making healthy changes on their own. These coaches become models in the area of self-awareness and can engage in a caring relationship with the person being coached. People who enjoy this type of work have to complete one of the many health coaching certification programs offered, either online or in a traditional classroom.

People who are already licensed health care providers can train to be health coaches, but this isn't a certification in health coaching. The types of professionals who seek our training include; physicians, nurses, health care administrators, physical therapists, massage therapists, pastoral care associates, psychotherapists, and social workers. This training can take anywhere from several weeks to a more comprehensive 12-month program and it also includes many classes that are necessary for certification.

The certification program may include specific training

modules that must be completed, to gain certification for health coaching. After taking all the re*q*uired courses, there is an application for a certificate that must be submitted within the following year's time. Besides turning in proof of course completion and the application, there are a few other steps that need to be taken before certification can be achieved.

One online program re*q*uires that a person seeking certification must show proof that he/she has been employed as a health coach for 6 months or been paid for at least 60 hours of health coaching. An application fee of 250 dollars needs to be submitted, as well as the following; current resume, 3 references from professionals, sample contract for a client, written description of some sort of scope of professional service, and promotional materials.

Once all the proper documentation has been gathered and is ready for submittal, there is an evaluation of the skill that needs to take place. The person applying for certification will need to demonstrate the following:

- Understanding of how to practice emotional wellness

- Ability to avoid prescriptions and medical diagnosis
- A vision for what their practice will be
- Ability to be non-judgmental and work with this type of attitude
- Ability to perform a Health Assessment
- Understanding of several health strategies
- Ability to listen in both a somatic and verbal manner

The seven classes necessary for health coaching certification include a course on the fundamentals, skills needed, personal mastery, personal mastery partnership in coaching, the business of coaching, how to coach from an integrative health perspective, and the seven steps of change.

At least 80 percent of these classes need to be attended to gain certification. If any classes are missed, the person enrolled in the course must listen to the tapes of the missed class.

There is a lot involved in attending these programs; above is an example of just one, but the benefits are fantastic. Being able to help others through their feelings of powerlessness against the physical and emotional issues they may be going through is a great feeling. A certified health coach is generally more qualified and better recognized as a professional in the health and wellness industry.

Is Certified Health Coach Training in Your Future?

Undergoing a certified health coach training program can be very rewarding. There are many things in store for you if you decide to pursue the health and wellness industry as a health coach but before anything else, you have to know what a health coach exactly is, what his responsibilities are and what is expected of a good and health and wellness coach.

A health coach is someone who is tasked to help people in efficiently managing their health conditions and even some illnesses. Most of these conditions are chronic and are hard to handle. When you are a health coach, you are expected to guide your client in properly addressing and discovering their strength to deal with lifestyle and behavior changes. You are not tasked with diagnosing an illness or becoming a substitute for a physician's care.

A good wellness coach undergoes certified health coach training which provides a framework that they can use to assist their clients in identifying issues, concerns, and problems. These issues are often hindrances that stop the client from taking full responsibility for a different lifestyle and health changes that he or she should do to achieve wellness goals.

Like all other forms of coaching, being a health coach requires you to utilize various forms of goals for a particular purpose, identify obstacles as well as become a personal support system for your client. The relationship that you build with your client has an accountability nature and is focused on achieving overall wellness goals that are defined early on. The client defines these goals with the guidance from the health coach.

There are many definitions of what a health and wellness coach is. Some scientists describe a coach as one who practices health promotion and education in a schooling and instruction context and aims to promote the well-being of his or her clients. Achievement of different health-related goals, most commonly losing or gaining weight, is also facilitated by the coach.

A good coach motivates behavior change to make it easier for the client to change his or her lifestyle to achieve a clearly stated set of health goals. Client-centered counseling is also expected since it is a good form of eliciting change in the behavior of the clients.

Clients who require health coaches are often ready for change, which significantly decreases their ambivalence for lifestyle changes. However, they might meet obstacles along the way and may need their coaches to help them get back on track.

Health and wellness coaching is different from other types of coaching since it does not instruct clients what to do, but rather help them overcome obstacles and motivate them in case they lose hope in the middle of the change or simply get tired of the lifestyle changes that they need to do.

The core principles that govern health coaching include encouragement, motivation and health attention. The atmosphere that is set within every session with a coach is directed to the client and on different ways of paving the way to self-discovery and self-motivation to achieve a healthier lifestyle.

Coaching Business - A Way to a Healthy Body and Successful Life

As time goes by obesity is slowly turning into a huge problem the State faces. For most citizens, eating is more than a necessity. Some treat this as a hobby that you simply couldn't let go of, while others see this as a means to overcome depression and stress. In the United States, most of the food being offered is high in calories, causing the quick production of unnecessary fats in the body. The case of obesity in the United States rapidly increases each year, with a ratio of about 15-20 percent for children to teens and a blaring 74% for adults. These alarming numbers brought the creation of various facets of organizations that focuses on solving the big problem of obesity.

There are organizations designed and founded to support charities focusing on obese related issues. They also give support to clinical researches and studies regarding the particular area. One clear solution presented is through coaching business, where it does not only help solve health-related issues but also provides an opportunity to provide jobs and let the citizens earn money from helping their fellow citizens in need.

As obesity is an issue of health and fitness, the idea of coaching is to make sure that the people who are having problems with their weight will be provided with a solution to remove the excess weight. Coaching business may even come from your own experiences as you traverse the road to fitness and health. With weight and diet coaching business, you will be able to help other people find their way to getting out of obesity, keep yourself healthy and strong while maintaining your figure, and of course, earn money, as the opportunity presents.

This concept brings a lot of benefits to both the obese and the aspiring instructors through the coaching business program they are offering. With this type of business opportunity, you will be able to enjoy the activity you are passionate about, while at the same time helping others to live a healthy life. Moreover, it gives you a chance to earn money. You do not exactly have to be a trainer and be at the gym just so you could become a coach; you can do coaching business while you are at home, and simply supporting others, and help them boost their morale by cheering for them and constantly giving them tips.

The issue of obesity could be a very sensitive topic, especially if you are one of those who are involved in such a crisis. To solve this problem, patience and strength are required from you. The existence of a support group does not only give you tips and strategies to lose weight. They are also there to make sure that throughout your weight loss program, you will not feel any anxiety or inferiority on your body and feel confident and positive that you can do it and overcome obesity.

Health Coaching - The Key to Replacing Bad Habits With Good

Too many people are quick to take physical well-being

and fitness for granted until it is too late and they find themselves without it. It is a familiar story. No matter how many examples individuals see of the impact such things as lack of exercise, poor nutrition, harmful lifestyle habits and preferences and stress on the health and well-being, physical and mental of others, they tend to ignore it. They tuck it out of sight and out of mind, categorizing it as "someone else's problem" - that is until it comes home to roost over their door.

Yet, although you may have the best of intentions, it is never easy to replace old habits with ones that optimize both your fitness and energy levels. This is particularly true if you feel you have little or no support in the task. This is where a health coach comes into play. Health coaching is a wonderful way of helping us get onto the right track and staying there. The role of a health coach is to act as both your guide and champion. This results in a strong basis of motivation and makes it much easier for you to locate what you need to achieve your short and long term goals concerning health and fitness.

One of the biggest problems individuals face is their unrealistic approach to the problem. They set goals to improve their overall fitness and health or to simply address a specific health issue that is not probable. They are unrealistic and can make it difficult and stressful to achieve. This increases the level of disappointment and sensation of failure. The result is a resurgence of old habits. If, however, you work together with a health coach, you will be guided through a process of identifying, selecting and implementing distinct and achievable objectives. A life coach will also help you through the process and, in doing so you will ac*q*uire the basic tools you need to create for yourself an improved *q*uality of life.

Another problem facing many who wish to alter their current bad habits to improve their health and fitness level, in general, is the availability of what can only be termed as generic information. The guidance and instruction one can access tends to be applicable in a variety of broad or non-specific situations. This contradicts the individual wants and needs of every human. Where they come from, their situation and circumstance vary one-from-the-other. This is also applicable to what they need and hopes to achieve. It is obvious that if anyone wants to make progress, they need an approach that is tailored to their requirements.

It is the only way to motivate them towards a successful change. Health coaching is designed to look at every individual. It is not a one-size-fits-all approach. Health coaching allows everyone to feel a part of their transformation as coaches guide him or her through the steps necessary to address personal needs. Under a health coach, the program will fit in with the individual's own lifestyle including the demands of time and place.

A health coach is not to be confused with a personal trainer. An online coach cannot be there physically urging someone on to do more, eat less and direct the level and type of physical exertion. A health coach works on a different level. He or she guides the client through the sometimes painful process of discovering and comprehending what their goal is. A health coach helps a client realize and utilize his or her strength, motivation, and inner being to accomplish the goals at hand. This is more effective since it works on changing from within not relying on the rote directions from some external force. It is easier to obtain what we want when we are provided with the right tools, are truly self-motivated and have the support we require. If these are all in place it is much easier to make those changes in our life we need, finding motivation and determination to succeed within us.

Healthy Living & Lifestyle: Health Coaching: Invest in Your Future - Stop Sabotaging Your Life

"I ought to, I should do, I don't know how to. If only there were more timeless pressure, less stress, I'm too tired to try, I just can't do this anymore, why is this necessary?"

These are explanations, justifications, and comments that indicate you are still in the "victim" mode of your circumstances rather than taking charge of them. Now is the time to choose to become more disciplined and to move through your comments to better health or disease management. Healthy living for a healthy future is an investment you can't afford to make.

It's time to use YOUR mind over YOUR matter!!! Let your Soul's energy direct your Spirit's housing! It's your future!! This is not just about your weight loss, or a diet, or a diet plan, it's about a commitment to healthy living and creating a healthy lifestyle.

As a medical intuitive and distant energy healer, I deal with alternative emergency medicine cases, sports medicine injuries and lots of disorders and disease in day-to-day life. Each presents is own health circumstances to overcome. Addressing physical problems and determining the underlying emotional and mental contributions that direct the body to manifest the disease or life issues is one set of problems, having acquired health conditions is another. Sometimes a client's current "mindset", lack of knowledge, or lack of "get up and go", sabotages their welfare and puts their life and health at risk, or on hold. Years ago you went to the gym an instructor-guided you. Then came personal trainers, and now it's a health coach, life coach or life purpose coach. All of these health care professionals are trained to help individuals take charge of their health. Today it's a holistic (mind, body, and spirit) approach to wellness ie improving existing health conditions, life issues, and your routine. This broader approach to coaching creates and promotes a healthier life and lifestyle and hopefully prevents and keeps future health and life issues at bay.

Before a personal trainer was a luxury, today health care management is a great investment in your future. A well-planned healthy life management program is complementary to and integrative with your physician's treatment and regime. Major corporations are encouraging and educating employees to have a better way of life, which is a win-win situation for both. It saves employee 'sick days", and the employer's large insurance costs.

Good intentions and intermittent actions don't always culminate in change. Even when you are educated and given the tools to change your life, a health coach works with you over some time to see that you don't slip into the past "automatic pilot" life patterns and mindsets that manifested your original issues or undermines your current progression. By choosing and living positive attitudes and health behaviors, you maximize the health benefits of your goals, and you create lifestyle patterns that support and encourage well-being.

It boils down to the basic fact that you learn to use YOUR mind over YOUR matter and to use your Soul's energy to discipline and maintain your Spirit's housing The combination of your steadfast commitment and a health coach who is there to give you nudges, encouragement, and guidance when needed, can make the difference between a want to-be-well victim of your health issues, and an individual who does the best with what they are given, and lives their life to the Max!

Are You Ready to Start Your Coaching Business?

If you are planning to start-up a new coaching business, you will need to take steps to build your brand, optimize workflow, bring in new clients and increase revenue. Starting up a new business can feel overwhelming, so it is essential to carefully research the process to make sure everything goes as smooth as possible. Here are three things to consider in the process of setting up your own coaching business:

- **Identify Your Niche**

    Starting up a coaching business in a specific area is certain to achieve a more successful outcome compared to trying to market a generalized service. A full coaching business can be applied to most areas such as life purposes, relationships, health, business, and career. The ability to solve a specific problem will help to gain a lot more permanent clients.

If restricting business to a single niche at the start feels a little confining, you can start to expand your services at a later date when your business is established and you have built up a solid customer base. In the long-term, you want to establish your business as the go-to destination for solving a specific set of problems.

- **Claim A Solid Business Name**

In the process of claiming the right business name, you want to capture something that highlights the unique aspects of your service or simply you as a person. When it comes to brainstorming ideas, try to avoid limiting the branding and marketing options, especially if you plan to expand the services offered in the future.

A popular option with a coaching business is to use your name or a nickname. This is a great way to visually associate you with the services offered. A further practical reason to use a personal name is that is will simplify the process of purchasing a domain name for your website.

- **The Type of Coaching Offered**

A coaching business is a relationship-oriented service and many coaches prefer to work in a face-to-face environment. But, there are other options such as web connectivity which can be extremely convenient and gives a much broader reach.

A further consideration is working from a physical office or home. An office location for the business is certain to help give the professional appearance and certain to appeal if planning to host workshops or group coaching. However, the ability to invest in an office will depend on your startup budget. The option of coaching from home will appeal to many and has the obvious benefits of no lease contract, no sitting in traffic, and the ability to work odd hours without difficulty. But, it is essential to set up a separate home office area that does not impact other areas of your life, such as household distractions, dogs, kids, etc.

Things to Do Before Building Your Coaching Business

Are you seriously considering building your own coaching business? How prepared are you? Unless you answered 100% ready for that question, I suggest that you read this article until the end. Here, I'll tell you the most important things that you need to get out of the way before you start coaching other people online to boost your chances of succeeding.

Did you excite to start your very own online coaching business? Well, that's good. Let me just tell you that this endeavor isn't entirely exciting and lucrative; it requires time, effort, energy, skills, commitment, and hard work. What I'm saying is that the road can get bumpy. It's better to know what you can expect ahead of time. Keep in mind that you're going up against a lot of people and some of them are already considered gurus in their niche. So, you must always put your best foot forward to get a better shot at succeeding in this field.

Below are the things that you need to do even before you start your business. Having a good, solid foundation will assure you that your business will not be easily shaken in the future. **These are the**

following:

- **Honest Assessment**

First, you'll need to make an honest assessment of your skills, level of expertise, and capabilities. Are you sure you have what it takes to effectively coach other people? Are you truly an expert? Do people come to you when they need advice related to your chosen niche? You need to ask these questions to yourself because there are just too many self-proclaimed experts in the online arena today and frankly, the internet doesn't need another one. Also, you need to ensure that you know how to coach other people. You see, it's possible that you're an expert but you lack the needed coaching/teaching skills. If you haven't coached anyone before, I would say practice so you'll get an idea.

- **Know your Target Audience**

The next step is to know the people who'll eventually sign up for your coaching program. It's crucial that you fully understand their needs and demands. You also need to know their profile and their level of comprehension. Knowing them on a deeper level would empower you to make your coaching programs more targeted and more focused.

- **Know your Competitors**

Whatever type of business you're sinking your teeth into, it's a wise move to know the people that you're going up against. You need to know what they're doing to attract your potential clients. You also need to know the kind and the quality of programs that they're offering. You can learn from their strengths and weaknesses. Then, create plans of action as to how you can outplay them. The goal here is to keep your prospects from doing business with them as much as possible because obviously, that would mean a lost sale for you.

- **Know the Market**

Do not dive in unless you're 100% sure that you're going to profit from this endeavor. Know if there's still room for an additional coach in your chosen field. If the number of coaches is more than the number of potential buyers, this will tell you that you'll just be wasting your time building your coaching business as your chances of making a decent sale is bleak.

- **Understand the ropes of internet marketing**

In building a coaching business, you need more than expertise and great coaching skills to succeed. You also need to know how internet marketing works. You need to understand how search engines and other internet marketing tools can help you reach out to your potential clients. Don't worry as it's not rocket science. If you spend a couple of weeks researching it and interviewing experts about it, you'll get an idea in no time. If you want to speed up the process, go ahead and read ebooks and attend related seminars. Believe me, it's worth the time and the money as it's your ticket to make enormous sales.

- **Increase your Knowledge**

It's not enough that you know your chosen niche;

you must be an expert. You see, you can't coach other people unless you reach this level. So, before you think about building your website or before you conceptualize your programs, prepare yourself first. You can increase your knowledge by conducting extensive research, by interviewing gurus/experts, by doing experiments, and by getting the first-hand experience. The more information you acquire, the better.

- **Study and Analyze your Target Market**

This is something that you need to do when setting up any type of business. You would want to know everything there is to know about the market you're targeting. What kind of people do you want to serve? What are their specific needs and demands? Who are your competitors? What are their strengths and weaknesses? Does the market you're targeting still needs additional coaches? Are you sure you're going to profit from this?

- **Observe**

Most newbies do not know-how coaching programs are conducted by expert coaches. If you're one of them, I would recommend that you spend time observing. If possible, sign up for those programs offered by your competitors to get an idea. Or you can hire other coaches to mentor you. Some of them would be happy to invite you to their group coaching programs. Make sure to take note and understand the structures of each program as you'll surely be able to make use of that later on.

- **Develop or Enhance The Needed Skills**

You'll become a better coach if you have exceptional problem-solving, communication, listening, and analytical skills. You must also be aware of the best teaching methods so you can transfer your knowledge to your clients as efficiently as possible. Also, you must be patient and determined. Just like any other endeavor, the road to your success in coaching business can get bumpy but you mustn't give up.

Coach - Are You Interested in Growing Your Coaching Business - Or Are You Stopping New Clients

This article is for those of you willing and able to change. If you aren't ready to look inside and change, move on now because what I'm about to tell you tends to turn some coaches off.

What I'm about to teach you works and works so well that if you listen your coaching business will change and you will become a successful coach. But, I've had coaches tell me that "Naw! No Way. You can't do that!" It's called shooting yourself in the foot. Just because these people have never experienced results so good as this they are willing to walk off and say "no way."

And it doesn't matter what type of coach you are, life coach, business coach, executive coach, career coach, or whatever coach. This works. The ultimate message may be different, to connect with a slightly different audience, but, the concept works for any type of coach, and any type of coaching business.

I was giving a speech at a trade association when one fo the officers of a local consulting group notified me that if I was going to speak to their group he'd like to hear me speak. One of the things I said was that if everyone would follow this approach 30% of those that heard what you said would want to meet with you. The guy who had come to "check me out" was already pacing the back of the room, and walked out. When I talked to him later he said: "no way, that's all B.S. and you can't speak to my group." When I told him that I wish he had stayed around since 30% of that room that night did ask to talk with me afterward, and I'd even share the names with him, he still wasn't interested.

The blind leading the blind. So, do you want to stick around and hear "the rest of the story"?

The key to your success is "to stop selling coaching" and to start talking about what your customer wants and needs. It isn't coaching. Here are the ground rules that will change your coaching business results, and I'm not kidding.

Marketing... that works for your coaching business [the big *q*ualifier]... is never about you, your products, your services, or your processes. So, STOP IT. Don't talk about coaching, that's your product or anything else about you

I know that confuses the heck out of you, believe me, I understand. So, how in the world do you get around to sneaking your coaching into this? You don't sneak it in. We'll get around to that in a moment. Let's get back to this not being about you.

Getting Their Attention

Be prepared with a simple core message that doesn't talk about you much at all. Basically it says "I work with _____ who struggle with _____, and my clients get _____ [measurable results, this is the VALUE of the results, not just the results].

I didn't say anything about coaching, how I coach, or anything like that. This was a simple calling out who I work with, what they struggle with... and that clearly defines who gets results from me and who doesn't. If that person is the one hearing this message they WILL stop dead in their tracks and listen to the rest of what you say. And the rest is only telling them what measurable results (the value) they will receive if they are the ones struggling. And, that WILL get THEIR

ATTENTION. And that's ALL that you want at this stage. DO NOT try for more.

When you give that message you want only one response, "WOW, how do you do that?" And, guess what? You aren't going to jump down their throat with a long "what you do." This isn't about you. It's about them, keep it that way.

In any case, it starts with developing that message that will have them ready to jump on you. So if that doesn't happen, it's your message and it needs fine-tuning. It's very easy to fall back into the trap that marketing should generate a little interest. NO NO NO! Marketing that WORKS will have them CHASING after you! So, if that isn't happening, you haven't got it right yet.

But, now that we've got that message, hold onto it. The next step is finding someone to use it on, and we'll hold onto the message for just the right time.

There are a LOT of ways to find someone, but I'm going to pick one that is probably the hardest for you, and it was for me. I'm doing this for one simple reason, if you can do it within cold calling, you can do it anywhere.

Cold Calling

For instance, let's talk about making a cold call. (Don't panic, I don't like cold calling either, but I LOVE this.) There have been times I've gotten up to 75% of the people I've called to want to talk with me further or to set an appointment. Would you like to do that?

First, find some common ground. I use LinkedIn a lot. So, I'll look up my ideal customer on LinkedIn, look up their phone number in the phone book, and give them a call. When I call them, I let them know that I saw them on LinkedIn, and was looking for a _____ [name what they do]. Now, SHUT UP. You just turned this call upside down. NOW they are WANTING to talk with you. So, let the call go it's the natural direction. Don't attempt to throw in what you do (it's not about you, or your coaching). Keep the focus on THEM.

And I know you are holding that "killer message" but hang on to it for a bit longer. This isn't the time yet.

I hope you get the hint here that this isn't about you, your coaching or anything about you. Keep it that way and this will SHOCK you when you see it kick into gear.

Ask them about their experience with LinkedIn? How has it worked for them? What was it they hoped to get from it? And have they gotten it?

They'll likely say that it hasn't worked that well. Ask them, in that case, what have you been doing? Let them talk. They are now telling you what's not working for them, and COACH this is where you come in, you can help them with anything they are struggling with right? But don't jump on it quite yet.

And, you might interject, "oh, by the way, it's worked pretty well for me, would you like to meet over coffee? I'd be glad to share some of the things that have worked well for me, and let's also talk about how we might help each other grow businesses."

And you have an appointment. Your job during that appointment is not:

- to coach them to an answer, or to show them what you can do (that's about YOU. Remember, this isn't about you? or coaching?)

- to sell them coaching, or anything else

- Your job at that meeting is to:

- Help them, share with them, and give them whatever they want and need.

- Help THEM discover all of the reasons that things haven't worked for them, and what it would FEEL like and LOOK like IF they fixed it.

- Get their mouths watering for the RESULTS that THEY COULD have if they tried any of the things you've done for others.

And simply say, "Is that something you like to have? And what would that do for you to have it?"

Let them salivate and then give you their answer. A simple reply, "I can help you with that." and SHUT UP.

Somewhere, either during the initial call, or, possibly after you've sat down to coffee with them, they are very likely to say, "Oh, what do you do?" And you'll answer with a VERY BRIEF " I work with...." and if you are talking to one of those who have been struggling with that problem you WILL get a "Wow, how do you do that?"

But you WILL NOT spend a 1/2 hour answering what you do. You might say something like, "The best way to answer that question is to tell a little story..." and you'll give them another 30-45 second excerpt about a previous client who had exactly that kind of struggle, and once they tried what you and they had discovered together they ended up getting _____ [name the measurable results, dollars, and cents, etc]. And DO NOT go any further no matter how tempting it is.

Simple, say, "Is that something that you'd be interested in seeing for yourself?" Let's talk over coffee, and fall back to that original meeting, or schedule it now.

Whether you follow this exactly and get the appointment, or whether you use the original concept about (marketing is not about you, your products, or your services) and keep the focus on them, there are a LOT of ways to get in front of a LOT of different people. This is ONLY one. As I said, if you use the principle well in a speaking engagement 30% of the room may reach out and chase after you after the meeting. It does work.

Starting a Coaching Business - FAQ's Answered

I've been offering coaching programs for years. Along the way, I meet not just potential clients but also people who are eager to sink their teeth into this endeavor. These people are hoping to start their own business for several different reasons. Some are just fed up with office politics while others are ready to take a big leap and grab the opportunity to control not just their working hours but also their earnings. Well, whatever their reasons are, they seem to have the same questions about starting a coaching business. If you're on the same boat as these people, I'm pretty sure you're also looking for the answers I'll provide here so, just read on!

- **Question 1. Is it difficult to get started?**

Answer: Let me be honest with you and tell you that the answer is yes. But keep in mind that nothing's easy especially in the field of business. Expect that the road to success will be bumpy. However, you can make this manageable by simply doing necessary preparations. Before you get started, ensure that you have expertise in your chosen niche and that you have experience related to coaching. Also, ensure that you have all the guidance that you're going to need from people who have already succeeded in this endeavor. Having an in-depth understanding of your target audience, target market, SEO, and internet marketing would make things a lot easier for you.

- **Question 2. Does the industry have more rooms for new coaches?**

Answer: Okay, you'd like to know if there are already too many coaches. Well, the answer is yes. There are hundreds and thousands of coaches but not all of them are effective in what they're doing. Half of the practicing coaches right now are mediocre. What I'm saying here is, you don't need to be bothered with the competition in your chosen niche. If you're really good, no one can stop you from getting on top of this game. The secret here is finding your niche and striving to be known as the best in this niche. You wouldn't need to worry about your competitors then.

- **Question 3. What's the most effective way to promote my coaching business?**

Answer: This is one of the most important questions that you need to ask when starting your coaching business. You see, most coaches do not have formal training when it comes to marketing and advertising. What they've learned from school and seminars are focused on how they can become better coaches. However, you need to keep in mind that being a great coach doesn't guarantee enormous sign-ups. You need to get the word out there and you need to connect to your potential clients. The secret here is knowing what your prospects want, knowing where they usually go and knowing how to approach them in a way that they'll be convinced that they need you more than you need them. Keep all the information about your prospects when planning your internet marketing campaign and I can guarantee you that you'll never go wrong.

5 Things You Can Do Right Now to Jump-Start Your Coaching Business

If you are a coach that has not been able to get your coaching business to the level you would like, you are not alone! Many coaches graduate from coaching school and hit roadblocks to getting their coaching business to the level that they can coach full time. Here are five things you can do now to jump-start your coaching business.

- **Pick a Topic and Write a 300-500 Word Article About That Topic**

Your topic should educate, inform or solve a problem for your reader. Target the content of this article to your coaching niche and the struggles that keep them awake at night. Use this article as the basis to develop a ½-hour workshop that will identify the struggles your niche faces, describes the pain caused by that struggle, offers possible solutions to the problem, and calls them to commit to taking specific actions to solve their problem. You can publish your article at ezinearticles.com and quickly gain expert status in your niche.

- **List of Group**

Make a list of every group you can think of that could use a free speaker and make an offer to speak for that group. Send them a one-sheet promotional letter that describes what you will be talking about and how the audience will benefit from your workshop.

- **Join Three Networking Groups**

Paid and free networking groups are easily found with a quick internet search. Attend these groups regularly and ask to speak at these groups as well. Talk to people and have an introduction ready that tells them who you are, who you help, and how you help them.

- **Offer a Free Session to People in Your Circle of Influence**

Send out an email to everyone you know offering an irresistible free coaching session. Tell them that they can take advantage of the offer or pass it on to a friend. Be sure to include your email address so that it is easy to schedule the free session. Be sure to give you session a dynamic title like "A free goal setting coaching session".

- **Give Something Free Away on Your Website Or Blog**

Offer the article you wrote in step one or another valuable gift. Ask people to give you their name and email to receive the gift. You can offer a free article, eBook, or teleclass.

These methods will get you in front of your target-coaching niche so that can get to know, like, and trust you. People need to know you and trust you before they will coach you. When you give someone something for free, they begin to trust you and can see that you can help them.

How to Grow Your Coaching Business Using VIP Packages

Are you growing your coaching business with

confidence, flow, and ease? Or are you feeling stuck, not sure where to go or looking for a road map to help you get going and growing in your way? This week's article is about how to grow your coaching business using VIP packages. I want to help you create compelling ways to set your business apart and stand out from the crowd so you become more client attractive and business magnetic than you've ever been before.

First of all, my definition of VIP Package is not what you may be thinking it is. A VIP Package is your coaching services "packaged" in a way that becomes truly Valuable, Irresistible and Profitable, meaning you create a high-level package that is Valuable and Irresistible for your clients and Profitable for you. V.I.P. Package = Valuable, Irresistible, Profitable Package IS! When you have a VIP Package ready to offer your ideal clients (your tribe, your authentic audience), you NOT ONLY make it easy for clients to say "YES" to hiring you BUT ALSO attracts more clients, more impact and more income consistently. And the BEST part is you have a business building tool you can use over and over again for years to come! I LOVE that. It's very empowering and enlightening, isn't it?! How to Grow

Your Coaching Business Using VIP Packages

Here are 7 ways you can use VIP pkg to immediately grow your coaching business. So which of these applies best to you and YOUR business? And more important, which of these are you going to apply the Law of G.A.D.I. - Go And Do It, first?

7 Empowering Ways to Grow Your Coaching Business Using VIP pkg

- **Speaking to SHINE Your Brilliance**

Speak to shine your brilliance at an event, and even if you're not allowed to "sell from the stage." A great tip here is to share your passion, energy, and expertise and invite a significant portion of your audience into VIP Package clients.

- **Networking to Share Your Passion**

Network to share your passion, even if you don't have a product to sell or a program to offer. VIP Packages fill that gap beautifully, giving you a great return on your time invested in networking and connecting with people. (And you can eliminate those time-wasting "get to know you" coffee dates!)

- **Having 1-on-1 Compelling Conversations with Potential Clients**

Have 1-on-1 compelling conversations with potential clients, even if you don't have a client base yet and you need to generate clients and cash flow quickly. With just ONE conversation you can have a new VIP Package client.

- **Having a Life-Transforming Option to Link Your Free and Highly-Paid Offers**

Have a life-transforming option to link your free and highly-paid offers. You need something to offer that's between your irresistible free offer (IFO) and your higher-paid program - and it must be simple and easy for potential clients to say "YES!" to. VIP pkg fills this role perfectly! Plus, by allowing your potential clients to experience a VIP Package event, you can often transition from a single VIP Package event into a higher-level program.

- **Speaking to Sell Your Services**

Speak to sell your services at events that allow you to make an offer from the stage - and you want it to be simple and easy for people to fill out your offer form on the spot.

- **Working with Clients Online**

Work with clients online. You want to expand beyond your local market and work with clients virtually... but you're not sure what the steps are or what to offer. VIP pkg solves this challenge immediately, giving you a bigger reach and the impact and income boost you've been looking for.

- **Emails that Educate, Empower and Enlighten**

Send emails that educate, empower and enlighten. You're ready to promote via email, but creating a teleseminar seems like a BIG risk. VIP Package 1-day event experiences are EASY to promote with as little as 3 emails (even to a small client base). Let me share with you some bonus tips to support you to continue growing your coaching business using VIP pkg with confidence, flow, and ease.

- **BONUS TIP 1: Boosting Your Coaching Business with VIP Package Events**

Boost your coaching business with VIP Package Events. For example, you're offering free or low-cost teleseminars/webinars... but they're not paying off as you hoped. With VIP Package events you can boost your free or low-cost teleseminar/webinar impact and income. In VIP Package Profit Secrets, I'll walk you through this step-by-step formula and share my insider secrets. You'll love how easy it is... and how much reward and revenue you generate.

- **BONUS TIP 2: Bridging Your Passion to a Profitable Coaching Business**

Bridge your passion to a profitable coaching

business. For example, you want to offer high-end coaching or consulting programs, but it feels like a big jump for your clients to take. VIP Package experiences are the perfect "bridge" offer.

As you can see, out of all the things you COULD do to grow your business, VIP pkg is the easiest, the fastest and most profitable path for generating more clients, impact, and income (and to be honest, the most fun!)... no matter what stage of your business you're at right now.

Now let's get you started growing your own coaching business using VIP Packages by applying the Law of G.A.D.I. - Go And Do It - and get clients, get going and growing in your own coaching business today! The question is which one of these tips are you going to do first? Choose one and do it now! Success likes motion. The motion builds momentum, and momentum creates success. Got it?! Now it's your turn. Your time is now. Go and grow your coaching business using VIP pkg today.

Marketing Your Coaching Business Successfully

When you first pictured starting a coaching program you probably thought it would be easy and you would quickly create an income, however, it is highly like that you have discovered very quickly that coaching is a business and needs to be treated like a business. Just like any business, a coaching business is not a get-rich-quick scheme; it takes hard work to put together and keep together and takes constant marketing attention.

Perhaps you have some clients you are coaching right now and you are seeing a steady stream of income. However, you need to keep in mind that eventually these clients will move on and you will need new ones lined up and ready to go. It is essential that you continue to market your coaching business now, while you are busy with current customers, and not wait until they are done. If you wait, you will likely see a decline in income as you find new clients.

How Do You Get New Clients?

When you are already busy, finding new clients can be challenging. Here are some simple ways you can find new clients.

- **Ask Your Current Or Previous Customers For Referrals**

Without a doubt, word of mouth referrals are a great way to build your business. Offering a monetary incentive for a new client referral demonstrates how much you appreciate their faith in you and whilst a referral fee is not a new concept, it works for both offline and online coaching. However, you will find that many of your existing clients will happily provide you with a reference - simply because you do a great job for them.

- **Have a Website or Blog Where You Can Showcase Your Expertise**

People will go to your site to check you out and see what your coaching program is about. Ensure that you provide tips that show you know what you're talking about, but don't give away everything for free or you won't get clients.

- **Lead Generation On Your Website**

Lead generation on your website is incredibly important and having a special giveaway offer to collect names and email addresses of people who visit your site. These leads may be potential customers and by using Follow Up Emails and a regular newsletter, you can stay in contact with them. Also, it's really important to have a way for your prospects and clients to easily contact you, as they may have questions regarding your services.

- **Post Helpful Information And Answer questions On Appropriate Forums**

Another way to secure new clients is to post helpful information and answer questions on appropriate forums. This is a great way to build relationships, develop credibility as an expert, and gain trust. Be helpful on these sites, and you will find that people will come to you but directly and blatantly marketing will most likely alienate your readers.

Blatant marketing of your business on forums is frowned upon and can even get you banned - so be sure to follow the rules of the forum and see how others are posting and answering.

- **Get To Know Other Coaches In Your Field**

Sometimes an associate will decide to cut back on her client load, or has an emergency where she can't take on her next batch of clients - simply because of the relationship you have developed with her, she may refer these people to you.

Your coaching business not only needs clients to succeed, but it also needs good material. By good material - it should be what the client wants. Always take note of how coaching sessions are going, and always ask for feedback. That way you can tailor your program to your clients. You may think you know what they need, but it might not be what they want.

How Can You Run a Successful Coaching Business?

Many new coaches struggle to set up and run a coaching business as no-one tells them where to start. They face the challenges of learning a new skill combined with needing to know how to manage and market their business, get new clients and also make a decent living too.

People tend to train to become coaches because they have a passion to make a difference, and want to help other people to live a life they desire, but find it hard to live their ideal life as well. Often they have paid out thousands of pounds to study for a coaching qualification, but this alone does not mean that they can run a successful coaching business.

The truth is that many coaches give up because they cannot make enough money to live through coaching; they struggle to find enough clients to pay the bills; or they suffer from feast and famine, which then impacts their health, wealth and self-belief. Then they are not in the right mindset to be successful. It is not just a mindset that can affect these new coaches, they need to learn the business and marketing skills to be able to run a successful business. But the good news is that these skills can be learned.

Here Are Some Of My Top Tips For New Coaches Who Want To Run A Successful Business:

- **Credible Coaches Have Trained With A Reputable Coaching Body** - You do need to be a great coach to be able to run a successful coaching business.

- **Life Coaches Struggle To Market Themselves** - What is your area of specialism? Having a clear niche can help you to market yourself more effectively and share the benefits of how you can help your potential clients.

- **Develop a Vision For Your Business** - where do you want to be in 1, 2, or 5 years? When you start with the end in mind, you can make sure everything you do moves you closer to your goals.

- **Learn The Business Skills To Become More Successful** - Find yourself a mentor who has already created a successful business as you will be able to avoid the pitfalls and costs of getting things wrong.

- **Make Sure You Are Financially Sound.** If necessary, take a part-time job whilst you establish your business. Many of the top coaches took this action as they developed their business.

- **Get Out There And Get Networking -** Not only will you meet like-minded people, but you can also get access to great resources and may get some clients too.

- **Get Online -** Although a website is not essential for your success straight-away, get yourself a blog, get on Facebook, Twitter and Linked In to get known.

- **Find a Marketing Strategy That Works For You -** Do you want to speak? Do you prefer to write? Develop your strategy and take action.

- **Get Help -** Although you may want to keep costs down in the early stages, you will probably find that other people can do some things better than you. Get yourself a bookkeeper, an accountant, and a virtual assistant, as this will free your time to work with clients.

- **Don't Just Sell Your One To One Time, As This Will Cap Your Earning Potential -** Start to package your knowledge into products and coach one too many rather than just one to one.

How To Build Your Coaching Business With Testimonials

Many successful coaches build their coaching practices by using testimonials. But many others either do not use them or use them poorly. The fact is, a well-crafted, relevant testimonial can be a potent influence on your prospects.

But only if you know how to use them effectively. Read on to find out how...

What is a Testimonial?

A dictionary definition is: "A statement, usually written,

in support of another's character or worth; a personal recommendation."

Or more succinctly: A testimonial is a statement from a client that details the benefit they gained from working with you.

OK, So Why are they Important?

Testimonials are important as they rely on Social Proof - one of Dr. Robert Cialdini's potent factors of social influence. "Social Proof" is a psychological phenomenon that occurs in ambiguous social situations.

Under these circumstances, people who are unable to determine the appropriate way of behaving look to others for clues as to what is appropriate.

What Is Needed for Social Proof

Social Proof is one of the most potent factors of influence and involves seeing what others around you are doing.

We've all seen it before - we choose restaurants that are popular over nearly empty ones. The logic is that if the restaurant is full then it must be good.

The power of Social Proof is greatest, Cialdini argues when three things are true.

- You find yourself in conditions of uncertainty.
- Many people can be seen as engaging in a particular activity.
- You believe these people are similar to you.

Therefore, the more people there are engaging in a given activity, the stronger the social proof. Likewise, if the people are like you (dress like you, appear to be part of your demographics or psychographics, etc.), their actions will be more persuasive.

Social Proof & Coaching Testimonials

We can utilize social proof via client testimonials to gently persuade our prospects to buy our products and services. If we use these testimonials appropriately in our marketing, we can leverage the legitimate social influence inherent in our client's recommendation to grow our business.

Making Testimonials More Persuasive

We want to use testimonials that our audience can immediately relate to as coming from members of their group. In our case, this would be people like our target audience.

People who have already attended one of our programs, gained value and recommend it to others are likely to influence the others by their testimonials. So these are the people we want to ask. But what makes a good testimonial?

Good and Bad Testimonials

Dan Kennedy distinguishes 'Good-guy' testimonials from 'Outcome' testimonials. 'Good Guy' testimonials say what a great guy Alun is, but are non-specific. They may be flattering to you, but they're next to useless as a testimonial.

Outcome testimonials, on the other hand, are most effective when they are:

- Based on the specific results your clients gained.

- They focus on what happened differently after you coached them.

- Quantified in terms of money, time or both.

- Genuine, and appear genuine.
- Relevant to your target market.
- Voluntary.
- Made publicly.

So you want outcome testimonials in this form:

"I did X (a relevant thing for your clients to do) with Alun and the result was (saving of a specific amount of money, time, etc.)"

- Full name, location, contact details

Your Testimonials Must Appear Genuine

Now, of course, I'm sure you'll be using genuine testimonials, but they must also appear genuine - so the more specific you make them the better.

For example, "I made £17,312.53 in extra coaching income from just one of Alun's ideas" is more believable than "I made £16,000 after attending Alun's course."

Also a client 'AJ from Texas' is not specific, and sounds made up. Anthony Jackson, Bank Teller, Fort Lauderdale, tel: 605-224-1817 does, however, sound credible.

When to Ask

Robert Cialdini says there are certain moments when his principles of social influence are greatest. So we can make use of these moments when we ask for a testimonial.

He says that one of the best times to ask is after your client has paid you a compliment. Just ask immediately if they'd mind putting that in an email. Or if requesting an email is not appropriate, ask them to write it on a piece of paper.

Other times to ask, according to Cialdini, are after you've completed a specific piece of work, or after you've achieved a notable result. So this might be at the end of a seminar, teleseminar, coaching program or client breakthrough.

How to get Testimonials

So now you know what factors make a good testimonial. And you know when to ask for one. So what's next?

Ask for them! Yes, you do have to ask. And consider obtaining an audio testimonial.

But if you've done a good job, most people are happy to supply you with one. Just guide them to be specific.

And once you have the testimonals, in writing, or audio form - use them, and build your coaching business!

Testimonials can be a powerful means to build your coaching practice. You have to ask for testimonials - ask after your client has paid you a compliment. Ensure you get specific outcome-based testimonials, not 'good-guy' ones. Make sure they are and appear to be genuine. Get testimonials from clients representative of your target market.

The Ten Keys to Building Your Coaching Business Beyond the Next Level

When you sit back and think about your business, what are the questions that you wrangle with the most? Are they questions of expanding your business, of how to stay competitive in the market, of how to expand your operation to include your network of colleagues into multi-coach interventions in organizations?

You have been selling coaching services long enough to know that there are natural, seasonal cycles to the market and you've probably already found business development systems to support you as you ride the waves of that current. Maybe you've overcome the hurdle of building your business while billing time and sustaining the momentum of sales so that you can balance your time between doing the work and getting more work. Perhaps you've mastered the use of the Lessons Learned Meeting to cut your sales cycle time in half and expand the sale while serving the client. Now you want to define what is next for your business. Where are you headed? Survival is no longer the goal, now you can focus on growth. Or not. What is the next level for you? What would represent a *q*uantum leap beyond the next level? Do you even want that?

Whether you are an experienced coach who has built a sustainable business grappling with *q*uestions about where you'd like to take your business next, or you are seeking a selling system for building your business, you will need a systematic action plan that integrates three distinct domains: networking, marketing, and sales. Of course, the first step is to strategically assess what the next level of your business will look like. Do you know what you want to do and what it will take to get there? Are you doing all you can to create the coaching opportunities you want? Do you have a concrete, systematic format for developing new business and new coaching clients? Are you methodically implementing a strategic plan? Take a few minutes to explore the ten keys below to see where you might be able to perform a minor mindset adjustment to tweak your business development efforts in a way that will get you what you want for your business and yourself. None of these is rocket science or truly new information, however, you may not have thought of them in the context of business development before.

- How Big is Big Enough?

    To expand or not to expand? That is the *q*uestion. If so, how? Stop to think about if your business is big enough. That means you have strategically created an entity separate from your profession that can hold the systems, people, strategies, financial goals, streams of income, and outreach methodologies that will attract and create the business that matches your values, vision, purpose, goals, intentions, and dreams. Does your business serve you while you serve your clients? Are you leading your business, or is your business running you? If you trade your time for money without additional streams of revenue, then you are self-employed, which is distinct from being a business owner. Did you intentionally choose that? If so, and it has been working for you, is it time to explore what it would take to go from a self-employed practitioner to a business owner? Business owners focus their strategies on systems and people: there are two ways to make money...either people work for you or your money works for you. To build a million dollar coaching business you need to leverage other people. Do you want to manage people and create systems or do you find that by remaining more of a free-lance self-employed coach you have more flexibility to create joint ventures and alliances and partner with colleagues to expand your market offering without having to build a business to do so? Do you define yourself as a practitioner, manager, entrepreneur, or all three?

There are a few great resources that will guide this inquiry further: The E-myth by Michael Gerber,

Rich Dad, Poor Dad by Robert Kiyosaki, and the life out loud [dot]com website which has free downloads and free teleseminars that support financial literacy and strategic business building. If you want to multiply your income, you will likely need to change what you are doing. The business strategy you choose will determine the size of the business you can build, providing you have done the pre-work to clarify for yourself how big is big enough for you. Having said all that, I hereby permit you to not grow your business at all. It is okay to accept that running your own coaching business may not be the highest and best use of your coaching strengths, and you might be better served to take an internal position in an organization in which you can use your coaching skills with your peers and employees.

- Building Business While Billing Time We are all familiar with the frustration of the cycle that has us, as coaches, generate a full pipeline of leads that suddenly start to pop like popcorn, generating business that we then devote our time to delivering. While we are focused on client service and deliverables, we often lose our focus and momentum on marketing and sales, thus resulting in the discomfort of finding ourselves wrapping up projects or client engagements with no further gigs on the horizon and we must start all over again to build up the business development bench strength. "But, I'm too busy to do any marketing or sales now...I need to focus on being billable, and the time I spend selling is not the billable time". Does this sound like anyone you know? In a systematic business development strategy, you can utilize two strategies that will allow you to continue to build a business while billing time, thus cutting your overall sales cycle in half and expediting your acquisition of additional billable time while reducing the amount of time you spend in-between gigs. One strategy is the Lessons Learned Meeting as a business development tool, and the other is actively building your business through referrals. The Lessons Learned Meeting is a structured interview with your clients and key decision-makers in the organization that takes place in the middle of the engagement as well as at the end. It is a time to check in with your clients and learn from them what is working and what can be improved as well as a time to share with them what they can do better or differently to help you to do your job better. Typically, these sessions are a mutual admiration and acknowledgment fest, which is a fabulous time to:

> a.) ask for testimonials,
> b.) ask for referrals, and
> c.) ask what other challenges, issues, projects, or needs are coming up for your client so you can shift the lessons learned conversation into a sales conversation.

When interacting with your clients at any point in time when they express gratitude or appreciation for your skill and contribution, you can ask for referrals. There are three keys to getting referrals:

- Provide exceptional service.

- Express the importance of referrals to your business.
- Ask for referrals.

Of course, once the referral becomes business, you close the loop with a handwritten note or small gift to the referral source.

- **No One is On the Bench**

How do you actively stay competitive in this rapidly expanding market? Networking and business development are not spectator sports. Not only do you have to be in the game, on the court, out in the field, but you must think of everyone else in the world as also being in the game with you. There are no benchwarmers, which means that none of your interactions with any other human being is ever wasted. Every moment is an opportunity for building relationships, for speaking your vision to everyone all the time. Another critical piece of this mindset is to operate from the assumption that everyone wants to help you. This assumption will allow you to make big, bold, outrageous requests that will encourage and invite people to contribute to your growing business and blossoming self. If you are not networking all the time, what is in the way of that? Even if you spend most of your time with fellow coaching colleagues, they can be a great networking and business development resources for you. Staying competitive in the market may not be about competition.

Let's explore the competition for a minute. In a personal services business like coaching in organizations, even though you and all your would-be-competitors offer similar or even the same services (360's, MBTI, individual coaching, team coaching, situational leadership, presentation skills, etc.), so much of what you do is unique to you as an individual, therefore do you truly have competitors in your market? Here's a mindset that better serves coaches to expand our offering into organizations and be able to provide larger-scale interventions than individual coaches: I've heard it referred to as coopetition, an amalgam of cooperation and competition. The idea is one of collaboration with competitors or turning competitors into partners by building alliances and joint ventures as a business development strategy.

If you struggle with staying competitive in the market, identify those you perceive to be your biggest competitors and approach them to create coopetition arrangements that serve everyone and the greater good of the client organization. It is the old win-win concept that we facilitate our clients to attain...just applied to your business growth strategy.

- **It's a Numbers Game**

There is a process of sales. To leverage that process, it is important to understand the numbers involved. Typically, research shows that it takes ten phone calls to reach six people to set up one meeting. It takes ten meetings to get one client. That means that for some folks, they would have to call 100 people to get each client. If ten clients are considered a full schedule, that means 1000 phone calls. The sales process can take anywhere from 5 minutes to 7 years, depending on your circumstances. Your hit rates may be quite different from the general numbers mentioned here, but until you know and understand the numbers, it is very easy to get attached to specific outcomes and to take it personally when you do not get clients. Persistence and resilience are part of this game. I've heard that 80% of people stop trying to connect with a prospective client after their 3rd attempt, however, 80% of all sales are made after the 5th attempt to connect!

Recognizing that it is a numbers game will allow you to keep your pipelines fully loaded, and to create the bench strength you need to continually generate sales. The gift in this numbers game is that it removes any of those pesky attachment issues many of our colleagues face. It is nearly impossible to be attached to the outcome of sales if you have more leads than you can track! Sales are only frustrating and emotional if we do not have enough possibilities in the pipeline, therefore we get attached to needing each lead to become business. If you are actively pursuing five strong leads, you have time to think about each one and to pine, for it to work out in your favor. If you are pursuing 150 leads, it becomes very difficult to have high hopes pinned on any one of them, therefore freeing you up to focus on the sales process rather than specific potential opportunities.

- **Scarcity to Abundance: Shifting Your Money Conversation**

We could devote an entire issue of the journal on this topic. Are you undervaluing your experience and under-pricing your coaching services? Our executive clients take us more seriously if we are priced in league with them...how credible are you if your hourly rate is more along the lines of what their administrative staff earns? There is a scarcity mentality prevalent in our professional community. This scarcity thinking leads to coaches undervaluing themselves, their experience, and their education which leads to under-pricing coaching services.

There are scarcity mindsets and coaching belief systems embedded in our professional community and propagated in our coach training schools that set up coaches to not make money. One such approach is the concept of giving away free coaching sessions to lure in clients. In reality, this method primarily allows the coach to undervalue his services and to attract clients who are more committed to getting something for free than those who truly value the coach and the service. Once someone gets your services for free, it is very difficult to transition to paying high dollars for it. Do not diminish yourself or our profession by attaching a valuation of zero to our work. You can make a huge contribution to the world by providing pro bono services to those who cannot afford it, but giving it away for free as a sales ploy is inauthentic and gimmicky. Offer a reduced introductory rate, if you must, but stop giving away free samples.

I am continually amazed at the statistics I read about the coaching profession that estimates that fewer than 7% of coaches are making a living at it. Yet there is a small percentage of sufficiently abundance and prosperity minded coaches who are generating sustainable six-figure revenues through coaching, and even fewer who have successful business models such that they are doing multimillion-dollar coaching businesses. Financial literacy coupled with abundance thinking can help coaches to shift the money conversation in our profession.

- Helping Professions and the Conflict With Sales

  Coaches are not unlike the other helping professions. Self-employed doctors, lawyers, accountants, artists, and mental health professionals often sabotage their efforts to make a healthy living or amass personal wealth by not engaging in prosperity-generating mindsets. Often, they are not aware of and are not taught or trained in a systemic sales process, so they find themselves truly committed to helping others and hoping that that will be sufficient to attract clients. They have a helping mindset and are hoping for sales. Often they have a negative view of sales and perceive it to be about forcing oneself on others or pushing people to do something they don't want to do. Shifting to reframing their current sales mindset to one of helping and meaningfulness would allow them to integrate their commitment with sales activity. The other thing I see a lot of is that people may be excellent practitioners, but often they are not business people or salespeople. To truly succeed in business, we must be coaches who think like business people and we must consider ourselves to be the sales executive in our businesses. If we think of sales as helping others to determine if our services and products would be useful to them or not, we can begin to integrate our commitment to helping with our need to sell. Approach every sales conversation seeking ways to help, with no pitches, no agendas, no attachments to closing. You can feel good about selling if it's about making a difference with people, impacting leadership, or improving organizations in a global economy. Identify your current mindsets about sales and see how you can reframe sales to align with your values.

- Asking for What You Want

    Closing the deal becomes very simple...almost a non-event if you've been fully present in the conversation. It is a matter of listening for the opportunity to ask for what you want. Yes, you have to ask for "buy". You have to ask your client to contact you. You have to ask for the money. However, if you have been selling through your natural style, using a coaching approach to sales, having an abundance mentality, and a helping mindset, then closing is as effortless as falling off a log. If you find that you have blocks when it comes to closing deals, then I'd refer you back to number 6 above and suggest that producing for yourself a shift in your money conversation will allow you to generate a breakthrough in asking for and getting what you want. The hardest part is knowing what you want. If you know what you want, then take the risk to ask for it. If you are not crystal clear about what you want, don't ask for anything until you attain that clarity, because you will only confuse yourself and cloud the energy flow.

- Thinking Big, Playing Big

    Once you've removed your blocks and left scarcity thinking behind, it is time to invent. Without the shackles of thinking small, what's possible? Can you double your rates? Can you re-think your sales strategy? Can you transition to a new business model? If the restraints are off...what do you want? Do you have a coaching practice or are you building a coaching business? How big is a big enough business? Do you have the right team around you to build something that will continue to support you, sustain your continual learning and development, allow you to focus on continual improvement in the areas of customer service and product development? Are you working as much or as little as you wish? Do you love all your clients? If you could have anything in your coaching business, what would it be? What will it take to get there from here? What would it look like if your business surpassed even your own wildest dreams?

- Harness the Sales Process

Knowing that sales are a process, respecting the numbers involved, and increasing your awareness of your own sales cycle will allow you to leverage the information in this article to take your business to the next level. To truly harness the sales process there are three things re**q**uired:

- Work the system,
- Be in continual action.

It is also critical to understand the distinctions between networking, marketing, and sales so that you can track your progress in all three areas. It takes activity in all three domains to produce dollars, clients, and business.

Networking involves all the steps you take to meet people and begin to develop relationships. Marketing is all the stuff you do communicate your credibility and service offering to the world. Making calls, scheduling meetings with those in your target list, and asking for the "buy" are sales activities.

- Mailbox Money

    Eventually, we get tired of selling our time for money. It is only so big you can grow your business that way because time is limited to 24 hours in a day and you are limited in how many of those hours of each of your days you can sell. The answer is to find multiple streams of coaching income, and multiple revenue sources outside of coaching as well. Perhaps you create products that leverage core content in a specific niche market, perhaps you catch the wave of the current trend to harness the internet to reach prospective clients and sell products. Perhaps you have secured an in-house position to utilize your coaching mastery, or you've branched into real estate or other investment strategies to put your money to work for you. If you are not thinking about or doing anything to generate passive income, that is - money that you earn that is not directly linked to an exchange for your time, then you might consider one or more of these avenues to take your business to the next level. How can you leverage those teleclasses you lead? Can you videotape yourself next time you are in front of the room leading a meeting or training session? Can you find a colleague to interview you on video or by telephone line that is then recorded and put into an MP3 file that folks can download from your website? Have you written a book or been meaning to? Can you take the materials that you have created for various client engagements and link them together somehow into a workbook or monograph that you can sell? Do all your products and services support a common vision, purpose, or set of values that you stand for? Where are you not accountable to yourself for what you and your business stand for and how can diversifying your revenue streams support that?

No matter where you are in your coaching business, there will come a time when you wonder what's next. Choosing which door to open next requires some reflection and inquiry. Often, the door we choose appears to be locked. We can momentarily see what's possible, and then upon setting out to achieve it, we find obstacles and hurdles to overcome. Perhaps the key to opening the locked door is one of the ten keys described above? I invite you to engage in a dialogue to raise the level of financial literacy and business acumen of our profession such that coaching businesses continue to grow and thrive in the global market.

How Can A Health Coach Help Me?

When was the last time you visited you, a primary care physician? Did they provide you with some recommendations, to eat better, or to lose some weight? Then I'll bet they sat down with you for about 40 or 50 minutes, explaining to you just how you should execute their recommendation, right? If your doctor didn't explain what you should eat, how to prepare it, what exercises you should perform, or provide with a blueprint for success, you're not alone. If your doctor spent 15 minutes with you, that is about the average time you'll get before they shake your hand and scurry off to the next patient. If your physician recommended you to a health coach they are partnered with, then your doctor is on the cutting edge of a new wave in healthcare.

Health coaches are one of the fastest-growing segments in the Health and Wellness industry today. They carve out niches ranging from emotional eating to single moms, who don't have time to cook. Health coaches provide patients/clients a sounding board for their issues and a platform to express their personal health goals and intentions, that normally are not found in most doctor's practices.

The relationship between a client and a health coach normally begins with a health history. The health history is confidential and provides the coach with basic information about the client. A typical health history will include personal, social, health, medical, and food information. If the client fills out the health history form beforehand, the health coach can review it before the session begins, but it can also be filled out during the session. Either way works well for most coaches.

The health history session will normally last around 40-50 minutes. It is sometimes referred to as an initial breakthrough or discovery session because the client has an opportunity to talk about themselves. This helps to build a relationship between the client and the health coach. When this happens, clients end up providing a wealth of information not only to the coach but to themselves. The coach's job here is not to just provide detailed recommendations, but to perhaps understand the root causes of the issue the doctor is treating, i.e. food allergies, or sugar addiction. Armed with this knowledge, both the client and coach can begin to set 1-month, 3-month, and 6-month goals.

It is up to the client as to whether or not they will work the coach. If they decide to work with the health coach, they will most likely meet every other week for 6 months. In between sessions, the client can email or call the coach, depending on their agreement, to ask questions and obtain clarity on the coaches' recommendations. The coach will provide the client with session notes, CDs/DVDs, food samples, and handouts. Also, some coaches will send the client's doctor a progress report every month.

Patients find that when they have achievable goals and a plan, recommendations to lose weight, lower their blood glucose, or blood pressure can be accomplished with the help, support and assistance of a health coach. So, can a health coach help you? The next time your doctor makes some recommendations that you're not quite sure how to execute, ask them do they partner with a health coach, and find out for yourself.

Health and Wellness Coaching - What's All

This Stuff About?

Several years ago, I had heard of coaching and even used a coach or two, but it was more for getting myself organized and getting my life pointed in the right direction. Like a counselor or a good friend (with expertise!), my coaches helped me to find perspective in my life and helped me get a clear view of where I was struggling. Once I could see the trouble spots, we were able to formulate a specific plan that I had to work and follow until our next meeting. At each meeting we'd review the previous one, discuss how I was coming along with my goals, troubles I might be having attaining those goals or completing tasks, and then coach on those or move on to new goals.

What I didn't realize is that the coaching I was receiving was helping to change me on the inside and my practice was then changing, too! I was becoming a Health and Wellness Coach. Today, I'm able to consult with patients and clients, to help them realize their health challenges, coach them to set goals for improving their health and well-being, and then chart a course with them to get them to where they want to be.

Here Is How I Explain Coaching:

Coaching is an emerging service profession based on concepts from sports, business, spirituality, psychology and organizational development. It's for passionate people like you who want more from their personal and business lives. A coach can help you set larger, more rewarding goals, develop a strategy to achieve them, and provide support throughout the process. It's not unlike having a personal trainer or an athletic coach... transformational, but in a business and personal sense. The achievement of goals is something that comes more quickly as a result of the coaching partnership.

With ever-increasing toxicity plaguing our environment, and a food supply nearly void of nutrients, we all must take responsibility for educating ourselves about the basics. Why should the foods I eat be organic? Why do I need supplemental vitamins, minerals, and herbs? How does my unique body chemistry, including blood type, metabolic type, age, gender, race, and personal history figure into my plan for achieving optimal health? Why should I avoid "wrapping myself in blanket statements" put out by the media regarding solutions to my various health issues?

When you connect with a Health and Wellness Coach, you align yourself with someone who can provide you with the answers to these and your many other questions regarding your health. You engage a professional who will help you discover all the areas of your health that need your attention, set realistic goals to achieve increased energy and vitality, and create rewards for all of your "little successes".

Health comes from you, not to you. It must be cultivated and cared for. Results will be steady, but you must know the path to take. So I suggest that you find yourself a Health and Wellness Coach; a person with the knowledge and skills to help you evaluate where your health lies today. Someone to set you on a path to take you where you want to be. You can self-medicate, but you likely can't achieve total health on your own. I urge you to take your life and your health seriously; to find someone who cares about you and can help you find the health and well-being you desire and deserve.

Health and Wellness Coach Training

Many training providers offer health and wellness coach

training. If you are aspiring to be a health coach and want to be trained by professionals, there are many things that you should look out for when looking for a good training center. These things will help you decide on the best training center that will teach you everything you need to know about this profession.

Most schools provide health and wellness coach training that are divided into core classes and support classes. Some many principles and skills are developed during the whole training and it's important to know which classes are important for you to decide on the school that will teach you everything you could need to become an effective health coach. Generic coaching skills are one of the basics of health coach training. Look over the curriculum and find out if the school provides extensive training in this particular area. Generic coaching skills involve several models and approaches to coaching. This gives you a wide range of options on how to deal with different clients who have different health issues and concerns.

Core principles in coaching must also be taught. Not only will this be very helpful in your future career as a health and wellness coach, but it will also make you more flexible and will prepare you to become a coach in whatever field you might find interesting in the future. Other coaching fields that you can apply with core coaching principles include life coaching, sales coaching, business coaching, parental coaching, financial coaching, and others. When you have learned all those core principles, it is of course very important to have courses that specialize in health and wellness. This is more specific and is a good complement to the basic coaching principles that you have learned in the first part.

Not only will this specialized coaching help you understand what needs to be done as a health and wellness coach, but it will also teach you how to help your future clients in changing their lifestyle and their habits. These courses will teach you how to help people eat better, reduce stress, exercise, quit smoking and make other healthy choices based on proven scientific approaches. Marketing is an important tool in health and wellness coaching. A well-trained wellness coach can attract clients and keep them in the program. A good training school should teach you basic and advanced marketing techniques that will help you attract clients without paying them and without massive forms of advertising on your part.

If you are checking out training providers, make sure that you choose the school where you can learn only from the best in the field. Review the people who will be teaching different techniques to you and make sure that they are qualified to be your wellness coach teachers. Schools that provide a certification program, whether affiliated to an institution or not, is also an advantage. Certification does not only check if you are qualified to become a coach, but it will also be an attractive part of your resume.

What Can Health and Wellness Coaching Do For You?

If you are like many individuals, there is something about your fitness level that you would like to improve? Perhaps you would like to lose weight? Gain strength? Eat more healthful foods? Control a medical condition, such as diabetes? The truth is, when we exercise and eat healthily we feel our best, and this positively influences all aspects of our lives. With a healthy body and mind, we feel we can take on the world!

It is often the case that we set health goals for ourselves but have difficulty in reaching them. Perhaps we need help in developing plans of action to achieve these goals. Or we need to reach deep inside ourselves to unearth the true motivators that will inspire us to obtain our desired outcomes. Maybe we are unsure of what our health and fitness goals are and we need assistance in creating goals that resonate with us. A Health and Wellness Coach is a certified coach who works with you to assist you in accomplishing your goals. Through insightful questioning, a coach helps you to create your vision and develop the steps you need to achieve that vision.

A Health and Wellness Coach Will:

- Meet with you weekly (by phone or in-person) to partner with you to help you reach on your goals

- Help you refine your vision of the healthy life that you desire

- Brainstorm with you to break down your goals into achievable steps

- Assist you in removing obstacles that get in the way of reaching your goals

- Support you in finding ways to be accountable to your goals

- Cheer you on in achieving your dreams!

Benefits of working with a Health and Wellness Coach:

- Coaching can help motivate you and keep you on track in reaching your goals.

- A Health and Wellness coach believes that you have the answers inside of you and will empower you to self-discovery.

- A Health and Wellness Coach is never judgmental and believes wholeheartedly in your ability to reach your goals.

- Most coaching is done over the phone. This is both convenient and a great time saver. It means that you are not bound by a physical location!

- A coach does not tell you what to do. A coach assists you in creating your own goals. This means that the goals you create are doable and geared towards your lifestyle.
- A coach is your partner in success!

A Health and Wellness Coach can help you reach your goals of creating a healthy, fit and strong mind and body.

Finding Out What's Right for YOU - Health Coaching

The newspapers, magazines television news broadcasts and even the internet contain daily some information or others about how our health and well-being are threatened. Yet, the message the research, pop-science, and advice are giving is very confusing and even contradictory. You should or should not eat eggs. Drinking low-calorie drinks is either good for you because they act to prevent tooth decay or bad because they are replete with carcinogens. The sun helps your body obtain vitamin D, but it is bad for you since exposure causes melanoma. How in the world can one person sort out the truth from the fantasy or completely bogus or over-reactive science? We need to do so if we want to minimize the risk of any potential harm and live a happy and healthy life.

A plethora of information, all claiming to be both accurate and the latest on subjects running the gamut from weight loss to sundry medical issues are available courtesy of television programs, newspapers, books, and magazines. Much of this has been proven to be not only poorly informed but also downright dangerous. Moreover, such articles never take into consideration such individualistic characteristics as medical history, the present state of health and fitness or even think about lifestyle. It stands to reason that what is beneficial for one person may not be for another. When you are dealing with your health, you do not need a one-solution-fits-all but a tailored response.

The current state of everyone's physical well-being, as well as alarming statistics on health issues and heightened awareness through the media, have resulted in more and more people stopping to consider their fitness levels and lifestyle. This has produced an increase in the demand for coaches in health. This provides people not only with the chance to access advice specific to their needs but also to have someone to back them up, motivate and provide support - an online health coach. This makes it easier to prepare and go through the necessary lifestyle adjustments to be successful. Whether you want to stop smoking, lose weight through adopting healthier eating habits, find the right way to deal with stress or even discover the best type of fitness program for you, online health coaching proves helpful for both short and long-term goals.

If you want to work with an expert online health coach you need to have or acquire certain skills. You also need safe and confidential access to such things as Skype or e-mail. A typical online health coach has a background in health services, nutrition or fitness. They frequently have received training in various areas of specialty including health counseling. Compassion and understanding make some of the health coaches and these experienced professionals truly want to help.

Health Coaching: Internet-Based Marketing Strategy for Modern Dinosaurs

Dinosaurs were still roaming God's great earth when I started lifting weights. Do you remember when sand or some kind of white powder eventually leaked out of the not-so-tight plastic cap on the 25-pound weight?

I didn't think so.

But I do.

We used picnic benches for everything: the shoulder press, bent over rows, the bench press, seated curls. Every once in a while, Mike, our garbage man, would drive, standing on the back of the truck, jump off and give us instructions. He was a well-built guy who got a major kick out of helping us. He was pretty smart about it too.

Today, some 40 years later, I look back on Mike's lessons, the physical growth experience I had from training and I find that it's easy to draw some parallels to developing an internet-based health coaching business.

I'll tell you what I mean.

Let's say, just for this article, that the major muscle groups are chest, shoulders, hips, and legs.

Further, the bench press is the basic chest exercise; the overhead press is the foundational shoulder exercise, and squats are the basic hip and leg exercises.

Now, I say, "Go and start with exercising every other day for 90 days performing those three exercises: the bench press, the shoulder press and the squat."

In 90 days, what would you look or feel like?

It's more than likely you wouldn't have changed.

"Why," you ask?

Because as simple as those instructions were, the execution wasn't easy.

Nobody taught you proper form.

Nor did you learn a muscle recovery diet.

Nobody told you about sleep, about proper rest and when it should be active rest.

When you decided on the number of repetitions, you did too many and couldn't walk or comb your hair for three days.

Nobody told you about supplements.

So after a week or two, you decided, "Heck, this isn't for me!"

But what if Mike was there for you as he was for me and my friends?

Sure, some of you would have still decided against this

type of training, but a lot more would have overcome the obstacles needed to get into shape and would have reached their goals.

There are a few lessons here: some principles that will never change.

- **Perseverance is one.** If you are determined to reach a goal and you find the right help, you will succeed (barring any unstoppable forces such as death).

- **Another is coach-ability.** You must be willing to take advice to reach your goals, not from everyone but at least from people who know what they're talking about and have your best interest at heart.

- **A third unchanging principle is a regular execution Action. Unless** you're a celebrity with deep pockets and a team of expert professionals executing your vision, then you'll need to take regular action -- just like building your body, it can't come overnight --to build a reputation through the development and demonstration of great content, drive interested people to your landing page, give them something they find appealing and valuable, and then sell them on a training, a product or a coaching program that helps them overcome a problem they're struggling with.

Sure, today's dinosaurs have laptops and iPhones, but the successful ones employ, among other strategies, undying principles to succeed. To become a great health coach using an internet-based marketing strategy, build a business that lasts. Knowing that it will take perseverance, coach-ability and regular action.

Realizing Health-Oriented Goals Through Health Coaching

Health coaching is a method used that's becoming more and more recognizable to almost all health care delivery systems - hospitals, health clinics and facilities, healthcare companies, and medical and nursing schools that's geared towards the improvement and maintenance of one's health and the management of an individual's infirmity and health conditions, especially those having chronic illnesses by means of lifestyle and positive behavioral changes. It is an organized and well-defined relationship between the patient and the health advocate, also known as the health coach that productively stimulates the participant to make necessary changes in their conduct using helping the client in exploring and resolving their indecisiveness in a behavioral change to achieve optimum health.

Health coaching is a lot more different than providing health teachings or health education especially if the concern here is bringing-about long term goals. Health teaching is the method used in imparting information such as how the disease occurred, the medication regimen, activity guidelines, and diet restrictions directly to the client, leaving him no choice but to adhere to the prescribed instructions based on his current condition through written home instructions, pamphlets, and booklets. Health coaching on the other hand, allows the patient to ventilate what's bogging him or her about his present health status and express his or her desire to what hindrances in achieving optimum health to get rid of and curtail to allow change of healthy behaviors, and what kind of health support does he or she want. Health coaching is client-centered, which means that its focal point is directed at addressing health issues and concerns that are only true to a particular situation in the patient's life.

As of now, the patients have the right to understand what their options in attaining optimum health are and they need health coaches with medical backgrounds who can interpret to them the complexity and the technicality of their condition according to their level of cognition and advise them the various ways on how to deal and make amendments in their lifestyle.

A health coach focuses on issues about the individual's standard of living and how to improve it. Health coaches do not function to formulate diagnoses, give a prescription to medications or to give health teachings, but they are there to guide, direct, and encourage an individual to identify and set attainable objectives that are vital in improving the quality of his or her life. It is a way of helping health advocates in motivating the patients to let go of their ambivalence, making them ready to make the behavior change and embolden them to take control of the precipitating risk factors and seek the appropriate course of therapy in addressing their chronic disease condition.

Health Coaching - The Real Deal

How many times have we all been to a lecture, participated in a retreat, we get all ra ra'd up, and then thud... back to reality, and your current reality is not your physiological happy place. Despair is a devastating emotion. We have all done it. There is very often a huge difference in theory & reality. We all know somebody who knows all the textbook rhetoric, but there are is an endless loop "but, but, but" why this knowledge is not applicable in their case.

Our health is worth everything. Let's face it - what good are we to ourselves, our families & our company if we don't have our health. According to the CDC - Center for Disease Control - 75% of our chronic diseases are preventable through lifestyle modification - but we have to make sure we modify those aspects of our health - otherwise, we are not improving our health. And of course... we need to find a program that will fit into our crazy hectic schedules, our likes, medical risk factors... there is an array of specific needs to be met to assure a successful program.

Time. This seems to be the universal scapegoat for not getting exercise, healthy food preparation... time is an excuse - & the right program for you will address this constraint. A study done by the American Heart Association in 2011 proved that remote health coaching can be just as effective as in-person coaching in improving measures that are potential contributors to heart disease.

There are a plethora of corporate health programs that supply generic health information available from several websites. The true talent & worth of a health coach is one who looks at your current lifestyle habits, designs programs for you, and tries them out with you - working on that all-important implementation phase with you. Guaranteed, tweaking or back to the drawing board is inevitable. Once again, more theoretical rhetoric - if the try it out phase isn't there. Ever watch a personal trainer prescribe the same workout and exercises for all their clients. I sometimes watch personal trainers getting clients to do moves that are contraindicated to the client's obvious physiological limitations. Lunges are most definitely not for all and don't get me started on crunches. Yet, trainers have their repertoire of the old stand by exercises, irrelevant to the client's skeletal weaknesses.

Yes, we can encourage somebody to join a gym - but if

they are only going to go a couple of times a week - not cool. We need to design a lifestyle integrating physical activity throughout the day. We know it is our sedentary time that has become the plague of our time. The danger of being dependent on a gym is people think "OK I can't make it to the gym, so I guess I will exercise, tomorrow, tomorrow... " being dependent on a gym for our physical activity can be deadly. Desedentizing, physical activity programs need to be designed with that person's demands in mind. How bout a working parent who drops the kids off to daycare, goes to work, picks up the kids, makes dinner... they are excited to make it to an exercise class on the weekend - good for them - but it is not enough. A good program will deal with these challenges.

What if the person is in a stressful relationship - we know relationship stress can lead to many symptoms of metabolic syndrome leading to heart disease. Even if the person is fit - the relationship stress needs to be handled. What if the person smokes, thinks the only food comes from a drive-by window, spends more time on an airplane than in their living room, has 100 pounds of fat to lose, drinks excessive alcohol, is in a wheelchair, is concerned about disease prevention, concerned about cancer prevention, mental focus, has known medical issues... A good health coaching program will guide you through your risks, and lead you to a physiologically rewarding, proactive lifestyle.

An effective health coaching program will do a detailed assessment of your own medical needs & risk factors, lifestyle patterns & habits that need modification or elimination, and build that program that will be tried & true for you. And most of all the "R" in relapse is for reality - a good program will help you recognize the signs, and build a track, to get back on track. There is an appropriate health coaching program for you & your employees. Be picky, don't settle for prepackaged, or someone dictating to you what is available. Your health re**q**uirements are the determining factor.

Build Your Health Coaching Business Like You Would Your Home

The strangest thing occurred after getting our certificate of occupancy. We discovered that our Jacuzzi spa didn't come with a heater.
What?! No heater?

It was a really easy fix. "Can you tell me the purpose of a Jacuzzi without a heater," I asked the contractor? Embarrassed, he had one installed the very same day.

But the whole incident brings up a very good point when it comes to Internet Marketing: there may be one master plan but there are many and varied prints.

You see, the plumber had his job and his prints, the electrician had his job and his own set of plans. The carpenters, the landscapers, the swimming pool guy... everybody was working on their plans but the general contractor was there to make sure the whole process worked like a finely tuned orchestra.

There's a lot of detail in building a house and it's easy, I discovered, to leave something out.

In this same house, the contractor forgot to leave enough room for a staircase. Oh, that one hurt. But they installed an elaborate entertainment center when the plans did not call for one. We got that one for free, simply because it would have cost them more to remove it. Launching your own health coaching internet based business is not too much different. You have a training program and a coaching program to market. The different levels of preparation for those items alone are a home study course in and of themselves.

But you have those.

You have to sell those training and coaching programs but people don't know you even exist. So you have to attract them, and not just attract anybody, but people who want what you have. Do you use PPC, CPA, article marketing? Driving or attracting people to your site is another multi-hour course, or if you like, a different set of plans when building your health coaching "house".

Then, when they get to your house, how does it look? Is it half-built? Is the roof on it? This is your squeeze page or landing page. And it has your sales letter on it, a letter that explains how you can help your audience with their struggles and problems. How does that look? Does it resonate with your potential clients? That's another blueprint. They decide it is worth stepping into, stepping into your health coaching program and wham, you sell them on an "entertainment console" you don't need and may not even want. So you need to approach them and find out what they want. Once you discover that, you build your program to their specs (not yours).

When building your health coaching business, understand like building a house, that there's no way, no how that you'll have it built in a day. There's the foundation, the walls, the windows, the ceiling, the electricity, the plumbing, the landscaping and if you're lucky, the Jacuzzi with a heater. So don't even try to build it in a day. You'll give up. Instead, create your blueprint and work on one section every day: product development, content, sales letter, emails and telling the world about it. In a year from now or maybe even shorter, you'll have a full-fledged business.

Build Your Coaching Business - You Are Uni*q*uely Qualified For This - Discovery of the Unique You

You Bring Value to Your Perfect Clients because You are YOU...

"There are more people out there waiting to hear your message who can only hear it uniquely from you than you can ever get to in your lifetime." Jeff Herring

As you begin to discover and perfect your coaching message, method and promise that you will deliver to your perfect client I would like you to look inward. Spend some time taking a personal inventory of you.

Did you know that you have your energetic signature that was defined at birth, and *q*uite possibly before that? Throughout your life, your stories that you created and lived through are all ultimately designed to work towards your perfect happiness & abundant life. It's true! No matter what your journey here on this earth has been - every bit of it can work for your good.

Let me invite you to sit down with pen & paper (no not at your computer for this exercise, please. Just trust me there is a purpose in this) and begin to write about your wealth.

What? Do you say you have no personal wealth yet? Oh, but you do! Your life is rich with experience - both good and not so good. You have ac**q**uired knowledge, and you have both raw and developed talent. I'll just bet if you'd permit yourself, you could list many personal victories that you are **q**uite proud of. Go on, permit yourself to make a list of the "uni**q**ue value of you".

Let me give you some of the areas I would like you to think about as you make your list of what makes you so valuable:

- Knowledge
- Experience
- Talent

- Community (friends & family at large)
- Character & Values
- Divine Connection - Spirituality
- Relationships (close, significant)
- Health
- Finances

In each of these areas make an inventory list of what is unique to you. For example,

- Do you have a clear, intuitive connection with the Divine?
- Are you in tip-top shape and healthy?
- Are you knowledgeable about nutrition with a wealth of experience in how to eat to keep yourself in optimum health?
- Are you a gifted musician or artist?
- Do you tune in to the needs of others **q**uickly and pick up on what others miss?

Go ahead, spend some time with an open heart and ready pen. You might be surprised at what you might discover about yourself. Remember you are looking for the value of the uni*q*ueness of YOU.

Building Your Coaching Business on What Works - Not What Doesn't

Sounds logical, however, I've been told so many times that everything successful for me and the coaches I work with doesn't work.

Listen to WHAT Works, Not What Doesn't

Focus on what works, not what doesn't. Don't listen to those that say IT DOESN'T WORK, listen to those who are saying IT DOES, and then find out what makes it work. 90% of all coaches fail in a matter of months. Listening to 90% of the coaches that aren't succeeding about what isn't working is a recipe for disaster unless it is tempered with "finding the fix." Listening to even 10% that survive is nothing but "survival." D you just want to survive or find real success? Find the 1% or less, that are the coaches that have built a business of hundreds of thousands of dollars.

When I started my coaching I was told,

- Freebie, giveaway's don't work
- Websites don't work,
- Speeches don't work,
- Direct mail doesn't work.
- I've heard stories that this approach doesn't work for executive coaching, or that doesn't work for small business coaching or life coaching, but may work in another area of coaching.

I still hear those comments now, but nothing has changed....except that the very things I've been told don't work have become the core for very successful coaching businesses, mine, and those coaches I work with. And by listening to the wrong side it slowed my coaching business growth significantly. It wasn't until I started listening to the superstar coaches that I found that success comes from finding the RIGHT WAY to do those things, not by avoiding them.

Why Do We Keep Hearing "_____ Doesn't Work"?

Because it isn't being done right. There is a difference between doing the right thing vs the wrong thing, and doing the right thing the right way. You will still fail to do the right thing if it is done the wrong way....or with the wrong target market. The biggest mistake is not having a POWERFUL core marketing message, a compelling, gut grabbing message. If you are out there saying "I am a coach" or, just plain "selling coaching" you might as well *q*uit now. It won't work.

However, when you find the powerful core marketing message, delivered to the right market in the right way, it WILL work...BIG TIME. In today's market place people need help, they just don't know that a "coach" is the answer. Stop talking "coach" and start asking them about their PAIN, and where they want to go and help them find that they can find a solution with your help. (Notice I didn't say anything about coaching????)

Here's a list of the marketing activities I keep hearing don't work, and the potential results once you find your POWERFUL core marketing message. By the way, I keep hearing that "giving away" your wares has to be avoided. In reality, a structured approach of giving samples, leading to people wanting more and more, has become the core approach that has typically landed 20% to 70% of the people coaches touch. Failure to have a follow through and nurture those coaches touch is probably one of the biggest mistakes coaches make. Therefore, the statement "that didn't work for me."

- **Speeches** - Room of 40-50, 50-75% of the room want to at least meet with you, 1-2 clients from every 40 or so in attendance. If this hasn't been working...then find your core POWERFUL marketing message. Do you have 40 or more attend? Then work on your POWERFUL marketing message that is being sent to these to get them to your speech or seminar.

- **Seminars** - Freebie seminars, about the same as speeches.

- **Websites** - with thousands of people looking on the internet for coaches, if you are on a search engine, with a POWERFUL core marketing message landing 5% or more of those is possible. I've seen some web pages hit

40+%, but they have a POWERFUL core marketing message. Indeed, 99% of all websites don't deliver new clients. Does that mean that websites don't work...NO? It only means that the website strategy doesn't work. It either has no traffic...so build the traffic. Or it doesn't have a powerful enough message to convince those that do see it act on it. It may also not be following a strategy that LEADS the reader through that thought process to act the way you want. So, fix it. Find your powerful core marketing message, learn how to drive traffic, learn how to LEADS your clients to you.

- **Spending Time With Other Coaches -** Although I've heard that spending time with other coaches is a waste of time....because you should be out there selling and coaching. One of the greatest things.....EVER...for my business was staying in touch with other coaches, not just socializing, but coaching each other on building their businesses, brainstorming, mastermind groups with a focus on building coaching. Early on in building my own business, when working in groups of struggling coaches, I watched most of them drop out, but I learned from each of them what worked and what didn't. Always focus on what can be done to move the group forward, rather than "this doesn't work." I also found groups of SUCCESSFUL coaches, some of the superstar coaches. EVERY ONE of them I worked caused my business to LEAP forward by multiples. Even though I learned something from one, I kept learning more and more. I coach other coaches helping them build their business.....and guess what...I keep learning from them, even as they are struggling with their business. I've seen ideas that I passed to them come back with a twist that is 5-10 times greater than what I gave to them. I can't encourage you enough to create a coaching mastermind group.

- So what is the message I'm trying to leave here? If you've tried any of these and it hasn't worked. You do not have a powerful core marketing message. So, find it. Check out my other articles on finding your core marketing message.

- If you know that someone has succeeded using this or that approach then it's your job to MAKE it work for you, or at least find an approach that you can make work. Also, determine how well it worked for others and set your goals to work toward that measurable result. Many coaches try a little of this, a little of that and none of it worked, so they walk away and keep jumping from one fire to another, never making any of them work. PICK ONE, then dive in and make it work. Then make it work measurably as well as it has worked for others. (Isn't that what a coach does???) Get help from other coaches.

- Don't listen to those that say IT DOESN'T WORK, listen to those who are saying IT DOES, and then find out what makes it work. 90% of all coaches fail in a matter of months. Don't listen to 90%. Don't listen to even 10%, they are survivors, but do you just want to survive? Listen to the 1% or less, that are the coaches that have built a business of hundreds of thousands of dollars.

Do you want to learn more about how to increase your coaching businesses? I have just completed my brand new guide to coaching marketing success. You'll also get a free invitation to join a mastermind group of other coaches as they build their business. Hear what works and doesn't work.

Inspiration Vs Motivation Applied To Building Your Health Coaching Business

Of the number of things that inspire me, successfully helping others build their business is near the top of the list. When I fail at helping others, the dismal emptiness consumes me. Not sure which feeling motivates me more: avoiding the sheer anxiety of losing or moving more toward the boundless exhilaration of winning. Without consciously thinking about it, my heart and mind started examining the difference between inspiration and motivation.

Inspiration is a sustainable feeling based on core values, dreams and a sort of longing. We usually look for it in our soul mate, our God, our family life and our profession. My spouse is an inspiration of mine. Despite difficulties in our marriage of over 30 years, I always seem to want to please her. It must have something to do with the initial feeling that developed over the first few years. If you've been married for any length of time, then you know that it requires a sincere commitment to getting through and over challenges. Sure, that inspiration has waxed and waned but for the most part, it still propels me to please her in the most genuine and modest meaning.

On the other hand, Motivation is the set of inspirational units that keep us working to remain inspired. I used the example of my marriage relationship to explain inspiration, so let's stay with that to explain motivation. I am motivated to bring my wife a cup of coffee in the morning. That simple act begins the day with fraternal charity and helps her ease into the schedule with a short and sweet introduction. We get to talk a little and plan for the day.

Sometimes, I don't feel like bringing her coffee but I've worked it into a habit and the petty annoyances that may pull me in a different direction have evaporated by the time she's finished sipping.

My motivation has served my inspiration, and the world is better off. Believe me, if you had any dealings with my wife before her morning coffee (or evening wine, for that matter) then you already know that the world is better off. Let's transfer this over to health coaching. I bet that you got into health coaching for two reasons: One, you love the health field and how getting healthy has changed your life. Two, you love helping others to get healthy and change their lives.

You've been inspired!

To reach as many people as you can, so you can begin to change their lives, you'll need to stay motivated. You'll need to learn the layers and details of marketing yourself on the internet. That's a simple sentence that's filled with thousands of details. You need to peel that onion back, uncovering, understanding and implementing each layer until it becomes a habit. When you reach that point, people will wonder where you came from, but you'll know what it took and the inspiration you relied on to get there.

Can You Benefit From Health Coaching?

Health coaching is right for you if you answer YES to at least 4 of the following questions:

- Is now the time to do something to improve your health?

- Is your lifestyle unhealthy and out of balance?

- Are you sick and tired of being sick and tired, stressed out, and/or under-productive?

- Are you ready to make lasting, positive changes in your lifestyle such as losing weight, lowering cholesterol, controlling blood pressure, managing blood sugars, or reducing stress?

- Are you ready to commit to an honest discussion of your top health concerns?

- Are you seeking to create more overall satisfaction by bringing greater pleasure, engagement, and meaning to your life?

- Have other traditional treatment programs failed to improve your health?

Competitive sports teach us that individuals learn best and attain peak performance when they receive support and guidance from a knowledgeable coach. So why should we go it alone and regard our health--something that we treasure and that matters to us--as any less important? In short, Health and Wellness Coaching, an innovative alternative to traditional healthcare programs, is for you because when you're focused and know what to do, you can accomplish a lot in a short period.

There are several steps to the health coaching process:

- Intake interview and evaluation (includes a coaching readiness and starting point/goals assessment);

- beliefs and values identification and clarification;

- development of a personalized plan of action;

- measurement of progress toward goals;

- adjustment of strategies as needed; and

- continual re-assessment of progress.

Candidates for health coaching include those with a variety of chronic health conditions such as arthritis, asthma, back pain, diabetes, high cholesterol, high blood pressure, kidney disease, and obesity (to name a few), as well as those who seek relief from everyday stress, anger, and anxiety, and those seeking to meet the demands of Attention-Deficit Disorder.

A passionate and effective health coach knows from both personal and professional experience that to achieve success, you have to know where you're going and how you're going to get there--essentially, strategy and structure. "If you don't know where you want to end up, it doesn't matter which road you take" (Cheshire Cat, Lewis Carol). Your coach also should be familiar with research on health coaching. Investigators in a Yale study showed that "coaching is a highly effective and superior strategy in reducing total cholesterol and other coronary risk factors such as blood pressure, compared to patients who were prescribed medication but not coached." If you suffer from a chronic health condition and your physician has recommended lifestyle changes, then coaching can have a positive impact on your ability to control the advancement of your disease. Following parameters set by your physician and working as part of a team approach, your coach can help you understand your current lifestyle choices and how they negatively affect your disease, identify things that you can and are willing to change, and help create a meaningful plan of action that assures success. The goal is to help you begin and maintain new healthy behaviors that will improve your quality of life.

For reducing stress, anger, and anxiety, your coach will work with you to understand the thoughts, perceptions, and events that create stress for you. He will encourage your development of self-observation and self-awareness so that you can learn about how you respond to stressful events in your life, and then help you begin to recognize how you can best manage your stress. This will enable you to select and implement a variety of stress management tools and techniques and to learn how to incorporate them into your daily routine. Through this process, you will receive support you when you need support, receive motivation when you need to be pushed, and receive encouragement and be challenged to help you achieve the "less-stress" balance you desire in your life.

All in all, health and wellness coaching is not just for problems, but rather it is for moving your life forward, expanding your possibilities, and realizing your potential through the use of a dynamic plan of action that addresses old and new problems with new and vital solutions. As Albert Einstein once said, "You cannot solve a problem with the same thinking that created it in the first place." Coaching is very affordable and convenient because it occurs mostly by telephone and through emails, depending on your needs and preferences, with the flexibility to accommodate your schedule.

The Benefits of a Health Coach

Have you ever attempted to get into good shape but failed? Have you ever tried to implement a diet just to find it too difficult to stick with? Have you ever found it to be incredibly difficult to stick with an organized exercise regime? If this is your current situation, you should certainly consider hiring a personal health coach. Your health coach will not be able to guarantee that you will increase your achievements in these areas of health, but the best part about having a coach is the fact that they can help you keep on track when it comes to your health. Many people find it difficult to stay on track with their health strategies, especially when there is no accountability for their actions.

- With a health coach though, there will be a person tracking every strategy you utilize as well as every action you take to achieve your goals. A health coach will even track the amount of progress you are making towards your goals each week. Keeping track of your progress will be incredibly important when you are attempting to achieve specific goals.

- A coach for your health will also be able to guide you towards the most effective actions you can take for the goals you are working towards. Whether you are dealing with a specific health condition, or you simply want to get into better overall shape, a coach will be able to guide you in the specific directions you need to go to move closer towards your goals.

- The different actions a coach may recommend to you will include new diets, eliminating certain foods you are eating from your diet, specific exercises you can perform, as well as many other tactics that will increase your overall health.

- In general, a health coach's goal is generally focused on increasing the client's overall stamina and vitality. Other goals of a coach are generally related to the goals each individual has established for themselves. A coach for achieving good health will usually attempt to guide their clients towards the best actions they can take to achieve their personal goals.

- A coach may not be able to describe the causes of a specific illness or present a solution for a specific illness, but they will be able to move their clients towards a direction that makes them healthier all around. A coach may utilize meal plans to regulate the food their clients are consuming regularly.

- Another recommendation from a personal coach may be related to a specific exercise. Perhaps you are hoping to achieve better overall health. If this is your situation, a coach will likely recommend a solution that is similar to running a mile a day, or some other activity, that will certainly add to your overall vitality.

- One of the most important aspects of having a health coach is the fact that they will help you stick with your plans. Not only will a coach develop the strategies you must implement to become healthier, but they will also stick with you to make sure you are following through with the plans that have been laid out for you. It is this follow-through approach to getting healthy that is the most important step for achieving vibrant health.

Health Coach Salary: How Much Does a Health and Wellness Coach Make a Year?

Health and Wellness Coach salaries can vary quite a lot. The U.S. Dept. of Labor Bureau statistics reported that in 2010 that the salary for Health and Wellness Coaches ranged from $23,443 - $61,928 a year. Of course, a lot will depend on the particular career path you choose to take after having received your training.

There are wide-ranging opportunities available, from owning your own business to working for a corporate wellness program, to joining a physician's practice. The salary potential is quite variable. Indeed.com states that the median salary for a Health and Wellness Coach is $72,000 annually. However, many job listings you'll find in this field omit to add a salary figure in their career ads, so it may be difficult to tell as a job applicant what you can expect to make. The interview will be key. Also, keep in mind that the more education and experience you have, the higher your pay scale will be as an employee.

If you choose to go the route of an Independent or

Personal Health and Wellness Coach, as a small business owner, many factors that affect your salary are controlled by the parameters you choose to set.

For instance, take a look at these questions you need to address in your business:

- Do I want to work from home or meet my client in an outside establishment? If so, you eliminate office space costs.

- Do I want to work part-time, and have just a few clients a week, or would I rather work with as much business as I can reasonably keep up with, such as 70+ hours a week?

- Do I want to offer extra features and services to boost my income, such as online courses or printed materials?

- Will I be spending time and money advertising my services to generate business?

Those questions and more are just some of the things to consider when starting your own Health and Wellness Coaching business. They determine your overall yearly income.

Given these wide-ranging options, the monthly salary

could be anywhere from $200 - $300 a month to even earning $1,000's+ of dollars a month. Personal health coaches often have fees between $100 - $150 an hour. Some coaches do offer packages of multiple sessions at a lower per hour rate.

Another financial bonus is that when you own your own small business, numerous expenses are tax-deductible, giving you quite an advantage in terms of annual earnings. If you choose a different career path and prefer to become an employee as a Health and Wellness Coach, you may find that as with any occupation, the larger the role and responsibility, the higher your pay.

For example, if you work for a corporation as an Employee Health and Wellness Administrator (around $50,000 annually), your job will involve less responsibility than if you were a Wellness Program Manager (around $75,000 annually).

Checking with local job listings will yield varying results depending on how large and established the company or practice is, as well as how broad the job responsibilities are.

For other examples, Health and Wellness Coordinators at corporations typically make around $50,000 a year, whereas Consultants make approximately $44,000.

The Bureau of Labor Statistics does see an uprising career trend in Health and Wellness coaching. They also foresee that about half of all employers will have some kind of Corporate Wellness program active for their employees in the future. With predictions like these, a career in Health and Wellness does look to have a very promising future. You may find that a Health and Wellness Coach earns a salary you could be very comfortable with. Job opportunities in this area are certain to grow.

Conclusion

Coaching is a relatively new profession and at this time, it is considered the highest form of helping other people in realizing their goals or in learning new sets of skills. Coaching is the result and goal-oriented and can focus on any area of life; family, health, personal growth, simple living, intimacy, financial development, spirituality, business, and career.

Anybody, including you, can be a coach as long as you have a good track of record on the particular niche that other people might find interesting.

The basic principles involved in health coaching include the opt demarcation of objectives, establishing realistic goals, and also leading the patients towards the goals. It is nothing like conventional patient education. You learn how to interact with patients and know about their problems that affect their health and well-being. With a background in RN coaching, you will be effectively able to recognize individual problems and fix them immediately.

www.ingramcontent.com/pod-product-compliance
Lightning Source LLC
Chambersburg PA
CBHW060835220526
45466CB00003B/1120